W9-DGH-972

The
Psychological
Development
of
the Child

PAUL MUSSEN

Professor of Psychology
Director, Institute of Human Development
University of California, Berkeley

Library
S.W. Ok. St. U.
Weatherford, Oklahoma

The Psychological Development of the Child

3rd edition

PRENTICE-HALL, INC., Englewood Cliffs, New Jersey 07632

Library of Congress Cataloging in Publication Data

MUSSEN, PAUL HENRY.
  The psychological development of the child.

  (Prentice-Hall foundations of modern psychology series)
  Includes bibliographical references and index.
  1. Child psychology. 2. Child development.
I. Title. [DNLM: 1. Child development. WS105.3M989p]
BF721.M89   1979   155.4   78-26384
ISBN 0-13-732420-0
ISBN 0-13-732412-X pbk.

Prentice-Hall Foundations of Modern Psychology Series
Edited by Richard S. Lazarus

© 1979, 1973, 1963 by Prentice-Hall, Inc., Englewood Cliffs, N.J. 07632

*All rights reserved. No part of this book
may be reproduced in any form or
by any means without permission in writing
from the publisher.*

Printed in the United States of America

10   9   8   7   6   5   4   3   2   1

Editorial/Production supervision by
Lynda L. Heideman

Interior design and cover design by
Virginia M. Soulé

Manufacturing buyer:
Ray Keating

Prentice-Hall International, Inc., London
Prentice-hall of Australia Pty. Limited, Sydney
Prentice-Hall of Canada, Ltd., Toronto
Prentice-Hall of India Private Limited, New Delhi
Prentice-Hall of Japan, Inc., Tokyo
Prentice-Hall of Southeast Asia Pte. Ltd., Singapore
Whitehall Books Limited, Wellington, New Zealand

155.4
M97p3

To Ethel, Michele, and Jimmy

229010

Contents

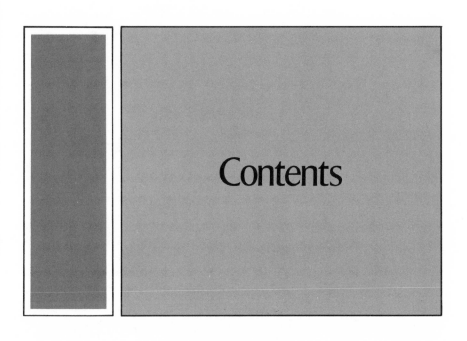

**FOREWORD TO
FOUNDATIONS OF MODERN PSYCHOLOGY SERIES**
xi

PREFACE
xiii

1

INTRODUCTION
1

The Goals of Child Psychology
Research Methods in Child Psychology

2

**GENERAL PRINCIPLES OF DEVELOPMENT
AND DEVELOPMENT IN INFANCY**
12

The Study of Infants
Characteristics of Neonates

3

LANGUAGE, COGNITIVE DEVELOPMENT, AND INTELLIGENCE
29

Language Development
The Child's Thought
The Development of Intelligence

4

PERSONALITY DEVELOPMENT: BIOLOGICAL AND CULTURAL INFLUENCES
53

Biological Factors
Socialization and Cultural Influences on Personality

5

PERSONALITY DEVELOPMENT: FAMILIAL, PEER, AND SITUATIONAL INFLUENCES
68

The Family
Peers as Agents of Socialization
Stability of Personality Characteristics
Situational Determinants of Behavior
The Modification of Children's Personality Characteristics

6

THE DEVELOPMENT OF SOCIAL BEHAVIOR
102

Social Behavior during the Preschool Years
Social Relationships in Middle Childhood
Social Patterns of Adolescents
Developmental Psychology and Human Welfare

INDEX
123

Foundations of Modern Psychology Series

The Foundations of Modern Psychology Series was the first and most successful in what became a trend in psychology toward groups of short texts dealing with various basic subjects, each written by an active authority. It was conceived with the idea of providing greater flexibility for instructors teaching general courses than was ordinarily available in the large, encyclopedic textbooks, and greater depth of presentation for individual topics not typically given much space in introductory textbooks.

The earliest volumes appeared in 1963, the latest in 1978 with the continuing expansion of the series into new areas of psychology. They are in widespread use as supplementary texts, or as *the* text, in various undergraduate courses in psychology, education, public health, sociology, and social work; and clusters of volumes have served as textbooks for undergraduate courses in general psychology. Groups of volumes have been translated into many languages, including Danish, Dutch, Finnish, French, German, Hebrew, Italian, Japanese, Malaysian, Norwegian, Polish, Portuguese, Spanish, and Swedish.

With wide variations in publication dates and types of content, some of the volumes have needed revision, while others have not. We have left this decision to the individual author. Some have remained unchanged, some have been modestly changed and updated, and still others have been completely rewritten. We have also opted for variations in length and style to reflect the different ways in which they have been used as texts.

There has never been stronger interest in good teaching in our colleges and universities than there is now; and for this the availability of high-quality, well-written, and stimulating text materials highlighting the exciting and continuing search for knowledge is a prime requisite. This is especially the case in undergraduate courses where large numbers of students must have access to suitable readings. The Foundations of Modern Psychology Series represents an ongoing attempt to provide college teachers with the most authoritative and flexible textbook materials we can create.

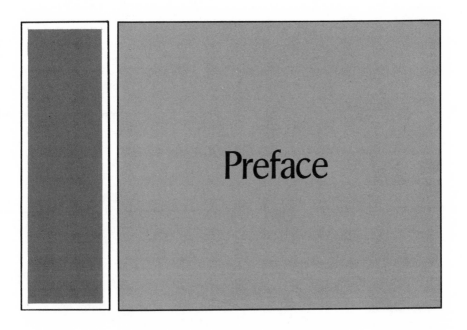

Preface

The third edition of this book, appearing six years after the second, focuses on the major theoretical and research trends in contemporary developmental psychology. In recent years, infancy and cognitive development have been the most prominent and active areas of research in child psychology. One result is a conspicuous increase in our understanding of the infant's cognitive capabilities, the nature of early social and emotional reactions, and the factors that influence these. Piaget's seminal writing and observations continue to generate many studies, but the scope of research in cognitive development has broadened to include non-Piagetian approaches to perception, memory, concept-formation, problem-solving, and social cognition. The problem of the effects of special training—including compensatory education—on raising the cognitive abilities of poor children has been a topic of considerable research interest. In addition, the number and diversity of investigations of language development have multiplied as attention has shifted from the acquisition of grammatical competence to the development of meaning, the precursors of speech, and the interrelationships between cognitive and linguistic development.

Although there is currently relatively less research activity on socialization and on personality and social development than there was 20 years ago, a number of highly salient and sophisticated studies in these areas have been published in the last few years. These deal with such topics as the learning of sex roles, familial determinants of children's aggression and of prosocial orientations, peer interactions and their influence on children's social behavior, and the impact of the media—particularly television—on development.

The results of recent investigations on these topics are summarized and discussed in this volume, as are many of the established facts and major theories of contemporary developmental psychology. Although a book this size can provide only a *sample* of these, the procedures of researchers in this field are stressed throughout—their general approaches to investigations, the formulation of questions and hypotheses, and the design and methods used in empirical studies. Furthermore, whenever relevant, the practical applications of research findings—for public policy, for the improvement of personal and social adjustment, for the alleviation of social problems, and for the reduction of tensions between people—are made explicit.

The book will be successful if it stimulates students to think more systematically about problems of human development and increases their understanding of the established and potential contributions of this field of study to the promotion of human welfare.

The
Psychological
Development
of
the Child

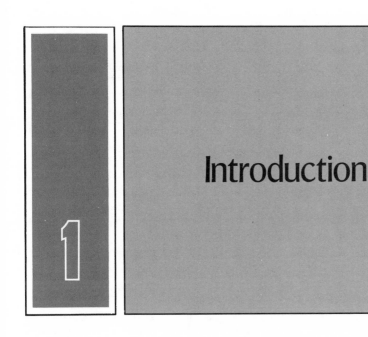

Introduction

The newborn nursery in the community hospital of the medium-sized West Coast city in which I live has about 20 infants. It is a wonderful place to visit. There are infants of different racial, cultural, and socioeconomic backgrounds—children of whites, blacks, Asians, Filipinos, native Americans; children of rich, poor, and middle-class parents. As you look at them lying in their cribs, you may be struck by similarities among them: they are all tiny and wrinkled, their legs seem very short relative to the size of their bodies, and their heads are relatively large. They seem defenseless, vulnerable, and helpless—although; in fact, all of them react to many stimuli and have many capabilities.

They can see, hear, and smell, and they are sensitive to pain, touch, and change in position. They are also capable of many activities and have a number of unlearned responses (reflexes). They cry, squirm, cough, turn their heads, lift their chins, grasp objects placed in their palms. They can follow a moving light with their eyes; their pupils dilate in darkness and constrict in light. A finger or nipple inserted in the infant's mouth evokes strong sucking responses.

You can just as easily focus your attention on the many differences among these newborn infants. Many are quiet and appear content; others thrash about and cry most of the time. Some seem tense, others relaxed. Some react very quickly to stimulation, others react more slowly.

It would be fascinating to follow the development of these children if we could. They grow at astounding rates in the early

1

years. By the end of the first year, their height increases by almost 50 percent, from an average of 20 inches at birth to 28 or 29 inches at 12 months, and weight about triples from an average of 7½ pounds at birth to about 20 pounds at 12 months. By then, many speak their first words and walk a few steps without help. By 2 years of age, most children walk smoothly and run awkwardly, and they begin to talk in sentences—very short ones, generally about two or three words. By age 4, their speech resembles the adult's in many ways. A 4-year-old's imagination is likely to be rich, and thought processes are much more complex than they were just 2 years earlier. And individual differences among children at later ages are more obvious and dramatic than they are at birth. Some children walk at 10 months, others at 18 months; some say their first word at 8 or 9 months, others not until they are over 2 years old. In any group of toddlers, there are those who are constantly on the move, exploring, jumping, testing things out, while others play quietly or sit and listen to music. Many play vigorously, laughing and giggling most of the time; others have a serious expression and cry easily. Norms of development are misleading because they specify only *averages* and tell us nothing about the great range of variability among normal youngsters.

THE GOALS OF CHILD PSYCHOLOGY

In reading the foregoing passage, you focused your attention on two central issues in the field of developmental psychology: first, general trends in growth and development of psychological functions, and second, individual differences among children. The fundamental goals or objectives of the field, stated very simply, are (1) to *describe* precisely and objectively changes with age in sensory and motor abilities, in perception and intellectual functions, and in social and emotional responses, and (2) to *explain* these changes and individual differences in ability and functioning. The developmental psychologist seeks to discover *how* and *why* these changes occur, to determine the underlying processes or mechanisms of growth and development. To illustrate, as a child grows older, memory improves, vocabulary expands, and thinking and problem-solving become more logical. Data on age trends and changes permit us to make some generalizations about the sequence and rate of development of these psychological functions.

Within any group of, say, 7-year-olds, there are intellectually advanced children with rich vocabularies and excellent problem-solving abilities, children who are average in these respects, and still others who are retarded relative to their own age group. What are the sources of individual differences? To what extent are they attributable to "nature"—that is, to biologically regulated genetic and constitutional factors—and to what extent are they the product of "nurture"—environmental factors, experience, training, and learning? These questions about the origins of individual differences among children are also basic questions that the child psychologist asks.

Explanations of age changes and of individual differences—of the hows and whys of development—are enormously complex and draw on findings from several disciplines and several areas of psychology: learning, perception, motivation, social psychology, personality, genetics, physiology, anthropology, sociology, pediatrics. For example, certain physical characteristics (such as height and rate of growth), intelligence, and some forms of mental deficiency and mental illness are at least in part hereditarily determined. To understand these fully, the developmental psychologist must know something about genetics. The striking physical and behavioral changes of adolescence are strongly influenced by physiological processes involving the endocrine glands and the biochemistry of the blood system; in investigating these phenomena, the psychologist must draw upon findings in physiology and endocrinology. Research in pediatrics has produced pertinent information on the effects of illnesses, malnutrition, and drugs on physical and psychological growth and change. Psychiatry has contributed many facts and theories about how early childhood events affect the behavior and adjustment (or maladjustment) of older children, adolescents, and adults. Many of a person's motives, feelings, attitudes, and interests are strongly conditioned by the social groups to which the person belongs, that is, by his or her social class or by ethnic or religious-group membership; anthropology and sociology have provided extremely valuable data about the impacts of these elements of social structure on personality, social characteristics, and development. Clearly, a comprehensive understanding of developmental psychology, of age changes and the mechanisms or processes underlying them, involves the integration of many kinds of data drawn from many disciplines.

Explanations of age changes in psychological functions are further complicated by the fact that various aspects of development are closely and intricately interrelated; developments in one function are likely to affect developments in another. For example, while children are growing and maturing physically (in large measure as a result of genetic factors), their intelligence is increasing and their abilities to reason and to think logically are improving. At the same time, children's personalities and social behaviors are becoming modified partly as a result of these physical and cognitive developments and partly as a result of their own social experiences. In turn, changes in personality and social behavior feed back on, and affect, intelligence and cognitive abilities. In brief, aspects of development interact with and influence one another.

For purposes of discussion, it is often necessary to isolate specific aspects of development, such as physical growth, intellectual development, or social behavior, and to focus on them separately. This gives a somewhat inaccurate picture of the developmental process. Therefore, the reader must constantly keep in mind the interrelatedness of *all* aspects of development.

In spite of the complexities and intricacies involved in understanding and explaining psychological growth and change, progress in the field of child psychology has been rapid and often exciting, particularly in the last thirty years. We have learned a great deal about children's physical growth, sensory capacities, and perceptual and cognitive abilities (including intelligence), as well as about age changes in these functions. Piaget, the brilliant Swiss psychologist, has given us superb accounts of the stages of development in cognitive functioning, beginning with the newborn's reflex activities and progressing to the adolescent's mature ability to solve logical problems and to reason. But the processes that account for the transition from one stage to the next are not fully understood, and many questions about cognitive development are still unanswered. For example, does a stimulating environment in the early years foster the development of higher levels of cognitive abilities later on? Can cognitive development be accelerated or improved by training, and if so, under what conditions?

The origins and development of personality characteristics and social reactions such as aggression, dependency, anxiety, competition, and cooperation have been the foci of a great deal of research. Consequently, we understand some of the principal determinants of aggressive behavior and know something about how such behavior can be controlled or reduced (see chapter 5). We have very little information about many other important aspects of the social development, however. For example, systematic research on "positive" social behavior—competence, independence, altruism, and sympathy—is just in its beginning phases.

This brings us to another important point about the goals of child psychology. Although *description* and *explanation* of development are generally recognized as the fundamental goals of the science, most child psychologists are also interested in the question of how the findings of their research and scholarship may be applied in improving the general welfare and the quality of human life. They want their research to yield information that is valuable in helping people to achieve better adjustment and happier lives, in facilitating effective learning and greater creativity, in reducing prejudices, fears, and anxieties, and in fostering altruistic, cooperative, humanitarian attitudes and behaviors. Consequently, much of the research in the field is concentrated on problems of social relevance, and the findings of such research have both theoretical and practical significance.

Consider the following problems that developmental psychologists have investigated. Ghetto children are generally deficient in cognitive skills when they enter school; that is, they score significantly lower, on the average, in language and intelligence tests than do middle-class white children. The factors that produce these differences may be discovered through research, and this information can be used in formulating programs to help prevent or overcome poor children's deficiencies (see chapter 3). Specifically, research can help to answer questions about whether preschool training can increase the cognitive capabilities of ghetto children. If so, what kind of training programs are most effective? Another area of vigorous research deals with violence, aggression, crime, and delinquency, which at present are major problems in the United States and many other Western countries. From such research, we have learned a great deal about basic mechanisms of personality development, and as we shall see, the findings are very useful in designing programs to ameliorate these problems (see chapter 5). The world would undoubtedly be happier and more harmonious if people were more considerate, cooperative, generous, and altruistic. If the conditions that produce and enhance these characteristics can be specified by investigation, the findings may be used by parents and educators to foster the development of these positive social behaviors in children (see chapter 5).

This volume reviews some of the most exciting recent research in child psychology, as well as significant, well-established findings from earlier investigations. We offer a well-selected *sample* of the major ideas, research techniques, and findings of the field. But a brief volume cannot present a complete coverage or survey of the content of the field. Instead, our aim is to present an accurate and well-balanced picture of what child psychologists do, how they conduct research, the facts they have discovered, and the social relevance of their research findings.

RESEARCH METHODS
IN CHILD PSYCHOLOGY

To understand, evaluate, and interpret research in child psychology—the *content* of the field—requires knowing something about how scientists plan their investigations, collect their data, and analyze their findings. Before turning our attention briefly to the matter of methods and techniques of research, it is important to emphasize that the phenomena that concern developmental psychologists are inherently complex and are multiply determined—that is, governed by many factors. For example, children's levels of aggression—or of curiosity, dependence, or altruism—depend on a host of things, including biologically determined predispositions, cultural background, socioeconomic status, experiences at home and in school, and the amount and kind of aggression they observe and copy. Obviously, no one can investigate all these variables simultaneously. Instead, an investigator ordinarily formulates some specific hypothesis or "best guess" about the effects of one variable (or, at most, a few variables) on aggression, and the research is then guided by this hypothesis. Suppose, for example, the investigator's hypothesis is that frequent exposure to violence on television raises the level of children's aggressive behaviors. Research would then be designed to test this specific hypothesis.

The fundamental general methods of child psychology, as of all scientific disciplines, are unbiased (controlled) observation and objective measurement. Observations may be made in *naturalistic*, or "real life," settings such as the home, nursery school, playground, park, or the waiting room of a doctor's office. For example, an investigator studying the development of cooperation in children of nursery school age might work with a sample of 20 children. In the method of time sampling, each of the children is extensively observed for several short periods (perhaps five minutes on each of four different occasions) as he or she interacts with others in the classroom or on the playground. The investigator would record all instances of cooperation between children, such as planning projects together, solving problems jointly, helping each other with tasks, offering suggestions to others, and sharing.

Other observations are made under standardized, controlled conditions, that is, conditions that the investigator sets up. Observations made under these conditions may be more precise and objective than naturalistic observations. If you were investigating the development of children's relationships with children their own age, comparing the earliest reactions with those of older children, you might choose as subjects 48 young children—12 (6 boys and 6 girls) at each of four ages (30 weeks, 40 weeks, 50 weeks, and 70 weeks). You could then bring the children in groups of three into a cheerful, attractively furnished room that had attractive toys and colorful posters and observe for 30 minutes how the children reacted to each other. The whole episode could be filmed or videotaped and then analyzed very carefully. Frequency and amount of such reactions as smiling, approaching, gesturing, playing together, cooperating, competing, and fighting would be noted. Comparison of the behaviors of children of different ages would enable you to make some inferences about age trends in early social interactions.

Whenever possible the investigator uses the most preferred method of scientific research, the experiment, to discover the reasons for changes in behavior. An experiment is another method of controlled observation, but it is distinctive for it always involves a controlled, prearranged *intervention* or *manipulation* by the experimenter. More specifically, the experimenter actually creates,.controls, and varies *one* particular factor—called the *independent variable*— and then observes whether and how some other variable (or variables)—the *dependent* one(s)—changes as the independent one is changed. Only one factor is allowed to vary at a time; all others are held constant, that is, not allowed to vary.

To illustrate, suppose we hypothesize that children with phobias about dogs (unusual, intense fear of them) will become less fearful if they observe other children playing happily with dogs and petting them. We could test this hypothesis experimentally by working with two groups of children with dog phobias—and it is not difficult to find a substantial number of such children. Children would be assigned at random either to an experimental group that will observe other children playing with dogs or to the control group that will not receive this "treatment." This would be done by putting each child's name on a slip of paper, putting the slips into a hat, mixing them up, and then drawing blindly an equal number for each group. Then we can be sure that the two groups are essentially equal in all respects at the beginning of the experiment; the groups do not differ in any characteristics that might affect response to the "treatment"—age, grade placement, sex, health, intelligence, socioeconomic class. We can then control the one variable with which we are concerned: observation of other children playing with dogs.

The children in the experimental group are then brought together for a series of four "parties" at which they are shown movies of a child playing with a dog. As the series progresses, the child in the movie becomes bolder, more vigorous, and more intimate in his or her approaches to the dog. The control group also has a series of four "parties" during which they see a series of movies, but these movies do not show children playing with animals. Following the series of parties, we could observe each child in a standard situation, bringing him or her into a large room where there is a dog and carefully noting all of the child's responses. If our original hypothesis is valid, the children in the experimental group will approach the dog without fear and interact with him in play. The control children, on the other hand, will still have their fears, so they will not attempt to approach the dog but will probably avoid him as much as possible. An experiment very much like this has actually been conducted with impressive findings that support the hypothesis (see chapter 5).

The most critical feature of the experimental procedure is that it permits precise and accurate evaluations of the effects of experimental treatments. Thus, in our example, we could measure precisely how watching films of fearless children affected children's fears of dogs. Without a controlled experiment, it is impossible to assess the relative contributions of each of the many variables that affect the development and reduction of fear—factors such as sex, social class, presence or absence of supportive adults, rewards or punishments for showing or inhibiting fear responses. Clinical and observational studies of fear reduction might yield valuable information about the influences of some of these variables, but these variables can be isolated and their effects precisely assessed only by experimental means.

Unfortunately, there are many important problems in child psychology that simply cannot be investigated experimentally. For example, it is important to determine precisely the effects of parental rejection on the child's personality development, but we can hardly expect parents to reject their children just so someone can conduct an experiment. Obviously, other methods must be used to study problems like this.

Parents can be interviewed regarding their child-rearing practices, the nature and extent of their interactions with the child, their expression of affection toward him or her, methods of punishment, and the amount of time spent doing things together. The interview data can then be analyzed, and parental rejection (or permissiveness, or punitiveness, or warmth) can be *rated*. These ratings of parental practices can then be correlated with measures of children's personality, derived from observations or tests. Unfortunately, however, the interview technique has many shortcomings: parents may not be good observers of their own behavior, their memories may be selective, or their reports may be biased.

Parent-child relationships may be assessed by means of another naturalistic method, the *home visit*. The home visitor, a trained observer, goes to the child's home and observes families in their normal interactions for a few hours on several occasions. These careful observations are the bases for evaluating variables such as parental warmth, rejection, permissiveness, or control. If, however, the presence of the home visitor inhibits the behavior of the members of the family—if their interactions are not natural or spontaneous when the visitor is there—the behavior sample hardly gives an accurate picture of family relationships.

Quasi-naturalistic structured observation is proving to be very fruitful in investigations of parent-child relationships. A parent and child are brought together in a standard situation that evokes interaction. The child may be presented with an intricate new toy or game to play with while the mother is given some magazines to read. The situation is likely to elicit a sample of habitual mother-child interactions, thus enabling the investigator to observe and assess variables such as the parent's ability to motivate the child, tendencies to guide or interfere, sensitivity to the youngster's needs and interests, use of praise or punishment, supportiveness, control, methods of enforcing rules, and permissiveness. At the same time, the child's reactions in a novel situation—independence, problem-solving ability, willingness to experiment with new responses, creativity, flexibility, ability to tolerate frustration—can also be measured.

As in the case in any young and dynamic discipline, new methods of research and measurement are continually being introduced into developmental psychology as old ones are improved or replaced. In recent years, these changes have enabled better, more systematic investigations in a number of critical areas, including visual perception and attention in infants, the development of cognitive functions such as memory and problem-solving, and the modification of personality characteristics and social responses.

Longitudinal, Cross-Sectional, and Cross-Cultural Approaches

Studies of human development may be classified as either *longitudinal* or *cross-sectional*. These can best be explained as contrasting methods. In the longitudinal approach, the same group of children is studied, tested, and observed repeatedly over an extended period of time. For example, in investigating longitudinally the development of reasoning ability and concept formation between the ages of 4 and 10, a researcher would gather a group of subjects and give them appropriate tests, first when they were 4 years old and subsequently at annual or semiannual intervals until they were 10.

Analysis of the results of the tests would permit the investigator to define age trends in the development of these functions.

An investigator employing the cross-sectional method to study these developments would give these tests within a short period of time (one testing essentially) to children of different ages, that is, to samples of 4-year-olds, 5-year-olds, 6-year-olds, and so forth. Comparison of the performances of children of different ages would, as in the case of the longitudinal study, enable the researcher to describe age trends in problem-solving and concept-formation ability.

There are several kinds of problems that can be adequately investigated only by means of the longitudinal method, however. For example, the study of *individual* trends in development must be longitudinal, for it requires repeated testing. We can determine whether personality, intelligence, or performance are stable, or consistent, over long periods of time only if we test the same individuals at different ages—a longitudinal approach. And we can most adequately evaluate latent or delayed effects of early experiences, such as parental overprotection, on later personality by longitudinal means—that is, by relating observations of early treatment to personality data collected later in the child's life.

Although it is very useful, the longitudinal method is extremely expensive and time-consuming, and it has some inherent limitations. For instance, we know little or nothing of how repeated exposure to psychological testing and observation affects the subjects in such studies or of the possible biases that investigators might develop as a result of their frequent contacts with the subjects. For these reasons, the method has been used only in a limited number of studies; the cross-sectional method has been used much more frequently in child psychology.

We must be very cautious in drawing conclusions about general or universal trends in development from either cross-sectional or longitudinal studies of American children. *Cross-cultural studies—* that is, studies of children in other cultures—may counteract overgeneralizations. To illustrate, according to the data from several investigators, anxiety and conflict, together with rebellion against parental authority and high conformity to peer standards, are characteristic of American and English adolescents. Many people therefore concluded that adolescence is inherently a period of stress and strain. Other data indicate, however, that in some other cultures—for example, in Samoa and in Israeli kibbutzim—adolescence is a relatively conflict-free period with little rebellion against parents or other authorities. Such observations help make us aware of cultural biases in our evaluations and interpretations of developmental data.

Hypotheses about "universal" or invariant developmental phenomena must be tested cross-culturally. Consider the hypothesis that what children express in their first sentences—generally spoken at around 18 months of age, regardless of the culture in which the child is reared—depends on their level of cognitive development; at this age, children are most concerned with movement and action, and these are the ideas they try to express. This hypothesis could not be tested adequately with a sample of first sentences of children of only one cultural background. Testing this hypothesis requires speech samples of first sentences, together with information about the context in which the sentences were uttered, from children in many cultures—for example, from the United States, France, Japan, Indonesia, Israel, Kenya, and Egypt. From an analysis of these language samples the investigator might conclude that, regardless of the language the youngsters speak, they are typically expressing thoughts about action and movement in their first sentences. Such results would constitute strong support for the hypothesis. The hypothesis would be rejected if the data showed that the content of first sentences varied from culture to culture.

General Principles of Development and Development in Infancy

Development is a continuous process that begins when life does, at conception—at the moment the mother's egg (ovum) is fertilized, its wall being penetrated by a sperm cell from the father. Immediately following conception, the process of *mitosis*, or cell division, is initiated. The fertilized ovum, a single cell, divides and subdivides rapidly until millions of cells have been formed. As development proceeds, the new cells assume highly specialized functions, becoming parts of various body systems—nervous, skeletal, muscular, or circulatory. The fetus, as a child is called before it is born, begins to take shape.

The sequence of development in the prenatal (before birth) period is fixed and invariable. The head, eyes, trunk, arms, legs, genitals, and internal organs develop in the same order and at approximately the same prenatal ages in all fetuses. Just about nine months after conception, the child is born.

While the processes underlying growth are extremely complex, both before and after birth, human development proceeds in accordance with a number of general principles. The most important ones are summarized in the following paragraphs.

First, growth and changes in behavior are orderly and, for the most part, occur in unvarying sequences. All fetuses can turn their heads before they can extend their hands. After birth, there are definite patterns of physical growth and of increases in motor and cognitive abilities. Every child sits before standing, stands before walking, and draws a circle before drawing a square. All babies go through the same sequence of stages in speech development: they babble before talking, pronounce certain sounds before others, and create simple sentences before speaking complex sentences. Certain cognitive abilities invariably precede others; all children can categorize objects or put them into a series according to size before they can think logically or formulate hypotheses.

The patterned nature of early physical and motor development is neatly illustrated in "directional" trends (fig. 2.1). One is the *cephalocaudal*, or *head-to-foot*, direction of development of form and function. For example, the fetus's arm buds (the beginnings of arms) appear before leg buds, and the head is well developed before legs are well formed. In the infant, visual fixation and eye-hand coordination are perfected long before the arms and hands can be used effectively in reaching and grasping. Following the *proximodistal*, or *outward*, direction of development, the central parts of the body mature earlier and become functional before those that are toward the periphery. Efficient movements of the arm and forearm precede those of the wrist, hands, and fingers. The upper arm and upper leg are brought under voluntary control before the forearm, foreleg, hands, and feet. The infant's earliest acts are gross, diffuse, and undifferentiated, involving the whole body or large segments of it. Gradually, however, these are replaced by more refined, differentiated, and precise actions—a developmental trend from *mass to specific activity*, from large- to small-muscle action. Babies' initial attempts to grasp a cube are very clumsy compared with the refined thumb-and-forefinger movements they can make a few months later; their first steps in walking are awkward and involve excessive movements, but gradually they walk more gracefully and precisely.

Second, development is patterned and continuous, but it is not always smooth and gradual. There are periods of very rapid physical growth—growth spurts—and of extraordinary increments in psychological abilities. For example, the baby's height and weight increase enormously during the first year, and preadolescents and adolescents grow extremely rapidly as well. The genital organs develop very slowly during childhood but very rapidly during adolescence. During the preschool period, there are sharp increases in vocabulary and motor skills, and around adolescence the individual's ability to solve logical problems undergoes remarkable improvement.

Third, complex interactions between heredity (genetic factors) and environment (experience) regulate the course of human development. It is therefore extremely difficult to disentangle the effects of two sets of determinants on specific observed characteristics; the

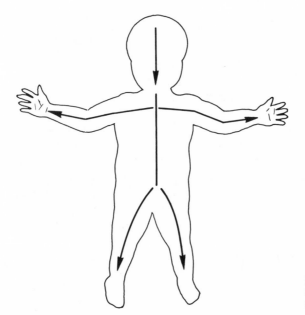

Fig. 2.1 Diagrammatic representation of directions of growth.

general question of heredity or environment is often essentially meaningless. Consider, for example, the case of the daughter of a successful businessman and his wife who is a lawyer. The girl's IQ is 140, which is very high. Is this the product of her inheritance of high potential or of a stimulating home environment? Most likely it is the outcome of the *interaction* between these.

We can, of course, consider genetic influences on specific characteristics, such as height, intelligence, or aggressiveness. But in most instances of psychological functions, the exact contributions of hereditary factors are unknown. For such characteristics the relevant questions are Which of the individual's genetic potentialities will be actualized in the physical, social, and cultural environment in which he or she develops? and What limits to development of psychological functions are set by the individual's genetic constitution?

Many aspects of physique and appearance are strongly influenced by genetic factors—sex, eye and skin color, shape of the face, height, and weight. But environmental factors may even exert strong influences on some of these characteristics that are primarily genetically determined. For example, the American-born children of Jewish immigrants two generations ago grew taller and weighed more than did their parents, brothers, and sisters born abroad. Children of the present generation in the United States and other Western countries are taller and heavier, and grow more rapidly, than children of earlier generations. Clearly, then, environmental factors, especially nutrition and living conditions, affect physique and rate of growth.

Genetic factors influence temperamental characteristics such as tendencies to be calm and relaxed or high-strung and quick to react. Heredity may also set the upper limits beyond which intelligence cannot develop. But how and under what conditions temperamental characteristics or intelligence are manifested depends on many environmental factors. Children with good intellectual potential, genetically determined, do not appear highly intelligent if they are reared in dull, unstimulating environments or if they have no motivation to use their potential. We discuss this matter further in chapter 3.

In brief, relative contributions of hereditary and environmental forces vary from characteristic to characteristic. In asking about possible genetic influences on behavior, we must always be concerned with the conditions under which the characteristics are manifested. In the case of most behavioral characteristics, the contributions of hereditary factors are unknown and indirect.

Fourth, all the individual's characteristics and abilities, as well as all developmental changes, are the products of two basic, though complex, processes: *maturation* (organic, neurophysiological-biochemical changes occurring within an individual's body that are relatively independent of external environmental conditions, experiences, or practice) and *experience* (learning and practice).

Since learning and maturation almost always interact, it is difficult to separate their effects or to specify their relative contributions to psychological development. Certainly, prenatal growth and changes in body proportions and in the structure of the nervous system are products of maturational processes rather than of experiences. In contrast, the development of motor skills and cognitive functions depend on maturation and experience and on the interaction between the two. In large measure, maturational forces determine *when* the child is ready to walk (fig. 2.2); restrictions on practice do not ordinarily postpone the onset of walking—unless the restrictions are extreme. Many Hopi Indian infants are kept bound to cradle-boards most of the time for the first three months of their lives and for part of each day after that. Therefore, they have very little experience using the muscles used in walking; yet they begin to walk at the same age as other children. Conversely, you cannot teach babies to stand or walk until their neural and muscular apparatus have matured sufficiently. Once these basic motor skills are acquired, however, they improve with experience and practice. Walking becomes better coordinated and more graceful as waste movements are eliminated; steps become longer, straighter, and more rapid.

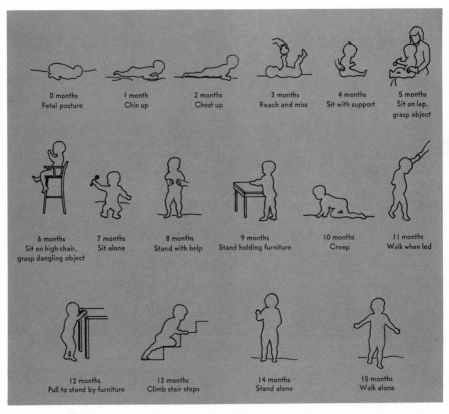

Fig. 2.2 The development of posture and locomotion in infants. *(From M. M. Shirley,* The First Two Years, a Study of Twenty-Five Babies, Vol. 2, Intellectual Development *[Minneapolis: University of Minnesota Press, 1933]. With permission of the University of Minnesota Press.)*

Language acquisition and the development of cognitive skills are also outcomes of the interaction between experiential and maturational forces. Babies do not begin to talk or to put words together until they attain a certain level of maturity, regardless of how much "teaching" they are given. But obviously the language that children acquire depends on their experiences—the language they hear others speaking—and their verbal facility will be at least partly a function of the encouragement and rewards they get for verbal expression.

Analogously, children will not acquire certain cognitive or intellectual skills until they have reached a certain stage of maturity. For example, until what Piaget calls the operational stage—roughly ages 6 or 7—children deal only with objects and events and representations of these; they do not really deal with ideas or concepts. Before they reach the operational stage they have not attained the concept of *conservation*—the idea that the quantity of a substance, such as clay, does not change simply because its shape is changed, for example, from a ball to a hot dog. Once they have reached the stage of concrete operations and have more experience with the notion of conservation, however, they can apply it to other qualities; that is, they understand that length, mass, number, and weight remain constant in spite of certain changes in external appearance.

Fifth, personality characteristics and social responses—including motives, emotional responses, and habitual ways of reacting— are, to a very large degree, *learned*; that is, they are the results of experience and practice. This is not to deny the principle that genetic and maturational factors play an important role in determining what and how the individual learns.

Learning has long been one of the central areas of research and theory in psychology, and many important principles of learning have been established. The discussion that follows is a very brief, and perhaps oversimplified, presentation of the three types of learning that are of critical importance in personality and social development.

The first and most traditional approach to learning is *classical conditioning*, the kind of learning demonstrated by Pavlov in the early part of this century. In his famous experiment, Pavlov harnessed a dog and sounded a bell whenever food was placed in the dog's mouth. The dog salivated, a natural, or *unconditioned*, response evoked by food in the mouth (the *unconditioned stimulus*). After the bell (the *conditioned stimulus*, which would not naturally evoke the response) and food had been presented together a number of times, the dog began to salivate each time he heard the bell; the conditioned stimulus had become capable of eliciting the salivary response. A new association had been formed between a previously neutral stimulus and a response.

Some of the child's learning occurs through conditioning, or the formation of new associations between stimuli and responses. To cite a simple example, a mother shows the infant the bottle each time she places the nipple in the infant's mouth; the nipple evokes sucking (*unconditioned*) responses. After several experiences in which the sight of the bottle is paired with the sensations of the nipple in the mouth, the baby will make sucking movements as soon as the bottle is presented. The child also acquires *avoidance* responses through conditioning. A toddler, exploring the kitchen, sees an attractive cup, reaches for it, and tips it over. The hot coffee in the cup spills and burns the child's hand. The cup becomes associated with pain, and on future occasions the child avoids reaching for it. In the same way, the youngster learns to withdraw from people who have been the source of pain or discomfort.

In *operant*, or *instrumental, conditioning* a response that is already in the child's repertoire is *rewarded*, or *reinforced*—by food, comfort, approval or a prize—and thus strengthened; that is, there is a greater probability that the response will be repeated. For example, rewarding 3-month-old infants each time they vocalized (smiling at them and touching them lightly on the abdomen) resulted in a marked increase in the frequency of the infants' vocalizations.

Many of the child's responses are modified or shaped through operant conditioning. In one study, every child in a nursery school class was rewarded by teacher approval for each outgoing social response and each instance of cooperating with or helping other children. Aggressive responses, such as hitting, teasing, shouting, or destroying things, were ignored or punished by scolding. Within a very short period of time there were dramatic increases in the number of outgoing, cooperative, and helpful responses; at the same time, the number of aggressive responses declined sharply. Thus, many personality characteristics, motives, and social responses are learned through direct contact with the environment that rewards certain responses and punishes (or ignores) others.

Complicated responses may also be learned in another way, by watching others: the child's behavioral repertoire is expanded appreciably through *observational learning*. This has often been demonstrated in experiments involving a wide variety of responses. In these experiments, children are exposed to a model who performs some action; these actions can be simple or complex; verbal or motor; aggressive, dependent, or altruistic. Children in a control group do not observe the model. Later, the children are observed to determine the extent to which they copy, or mimic, the behavior displayed by the model. Observational learning, the results show, is very effective: children in the experimental group generally imitate the model's responses; the controls do not exhibit the responses. Note that reinforcement is not required for either acquiring or eliciting imitated responses.

Obviously the child does not have to learn how to respond to each new situation. After a response has become associated with a stimulus or environmental setting, it is likely to be transferred to other similar situations. This is the principle of *stimulus generalization*. If the child has learned to stroke her own dog, she is apt to pet other dogs, especially those who are similar to hers. If her own dog is a small terrier, she is more likely to approach a miniature poodle than a St. Bernard.

Sixth, there are critical or sensitive periods in the development of certain body organs and psychological functions. Interference with normal development at these periods may result in permanent deficiencies or malfunctions. For example, there are critical periods in the development of the fetus's heart, eyes, lungs, and kidneys; if the course of normal development is interrupted at one of these periods—perhaps as a result of maternal virus infection or German measles (rubella)—the child may suffer permanent organ damage.

Erik Erikson, a prominent child psychoanalyst and theorist, considers the first year of life to be a critical period for the development of trust in others. The infant who does not experience adequate warmth, love, and gratification of needs during this time may fail to develop a sense of trust and consequently may fail to form satisfactory relationships at later times. Analogously, there seem to be periods of "readiness" for learning various tasks, such as reading or bicycle riding. The child who does not learn these tasks during these periods may have great difficulty learning them later.

Seventh, children's experiences at one stage of development affect their later development. If a pregnant woman suffers severe malnourishment, the child she is carrying may not develop the normal number of brain cells and may therefore be born mentally defective. Infants who spend their first months in very dull, unstimulating environments appear to be deficient in cognitive skills and perform poorly on tests of intellectual function in later childhood. The child who receives too little warmth, love, and attention in the first year fails to develop self-confidence and trust early in life and is likely to be emotionally unstable and maladjusted at adolescence.

THE STUDY OF INFANTS

For both theoretical and practical reasons, the study of infancy has become increasingly important since the early 1960s. Several of the broad general principles of development discussed above were derived from research with infants. Human development depends to a great extent on learning and experience. In order to understand these processes we must know the bases on which learning must be built; that is, the needs, sensory capacities, and response capabilities the individual starts with.

Of course, there are basic, innate biological needs—needs for oxygen, for food and drink, for elimination, for temperature regulation. The ancients were aware of the fact that neonates (newborns) have many motor reflexes (automatic, involuntary responses) that have survival value. These include *sucking* to get milk and *pupillary reflexes* (contraction of the pupils of the eyes as protection against bright lights or flashes).

Some new and exciting research demonstrates that the newborn is a remarkably capable organism and has much more cognitive ability than had been realized in the past. Almost from the moment of birth, the infant is able to learn, and some rather complex perceptual capacities and some kinds of understanding previously believed to be products of learning and experience now appear to be "programmed" into the organism. Before turning to these fascinating new findings, let us briefly survey the neonate's physical characteristics, needs, and sensory capacities.

CHARACTERISTICS OF NEONATES

Physical Growth

The infant's body grows extremely rapidly during the first year, when relative increases in length and weight are greater than at any later time. The baby's birth weight—about seven pounds on the average for boys and slightly less for girls—doubles during the first 6 months and almost triples in the first year. Body length, for boys about 20 inches at birth on the average, increases over one-third to about 28 or 29 inches by the end of the first year.

During infancy, different parts of the body grow at different rates until body proportions become more like an adult's (fig. 2.3). In accordance with the head-to-foot principle of development, the head and upper parts of the body grow at a faster pace than the trunk and legs. Head size increases at an amazing rate, beginning almost immediately after conception, and by birth the head is about 60 percent as large as it will be in adulthood. A newborn baby appears to be top-heavy, the length of his or her head being one-fourth of total body length. Brain size doubles during the first two years. The trunk ranks second to the head in overall growth rate, reaching approximately half of its full (adult) length by the end of the second year. Of all the parts of the neonate's body, the legs are furthest from adult size; relative to the upper parts of the body, they grow slowly.

Neonatal Needs

Many of the infant's innate biological needs are gratified in self-regulatory ways, that is, without voluntary control or active participation by the infant or by others. For example, reflex breathing

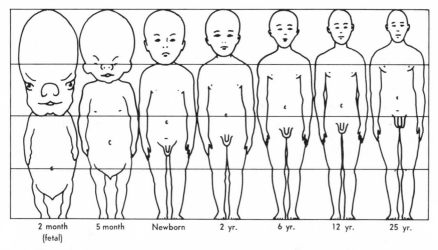

| 2 month (fetal) | 5 month | Newborn | 2 yr. | 6 yr. | 12 yr. | 25 yr. |

Fig. 2.3 Changes in form and proportion of the human body during fetal and postnatal life. *(From C. M. Jackson, "Some Aspects of Form and Growth," in* Growth, *ed. W. J. Robbins et al. [New Haven, Conn.: Yale University Press, 1929], p. 118. By permission.)*

mechanisms provide enough oxygen to take care of the neonate's requirements. Reflexes of the sphincter take care of the infant's need for elimination, and under ordinary circumstances automatic physiological reactions keep his or her body at a relatively constant temperature. The body's chemical and physiological balances, and thus energy, are maintained through sleep; unless infants are ill, in pain, or extremely hungry or uncomfortable, they will sleep as much as they need to and awaken when they are rested.

Two prominent biological needs, hunger and thirst, are not satisfied automatically. If no one helps the infant to gratify these needs promptly, tensions may become intense and painful. The social relationships related to satisfaction of these needs are among infants' most important early experiences and may have enduring effects on their later development (see chapter 5).

Sensory and Perceptual Abilities

Infants' sensory systems are remarkably well developed at birth. They can see, hear, and smell, and they are sensitive to pain, touch, and change of position. While their sense of taste is not well developed at first, they react to differences in sweet-tasting and sour-tasting substances within the first two weeks. Sensitivity to pain, already present at birth, becomes keener within the first few days. Coordination and convergence of the eyes, required for visual fixation and for depth perception, begin to develop immediately after

21

birth and appear to be fairly well established by the age of 7 or 8 weeks. Infants as young as 15 days of age can discriminate differences in brightness and hue. Swing a bright object before infants or project a moving colored spot on the ceiling above, and they will follow it with their eyes.

Since newborns' sensory organs function well, they are sensitive to many stimuli. But they do not attend to everything equally; they focus attention much more on some stimuli than on others. Stimuli with a "high rate of change"—those that move, or have marked contrasts between light and dark, or have a great deal of contour (black edge on white background)—are likely to attract and hold newborns' attentions. When their eyes are open, they search until they find some contour edges, and then they focus on these edges. Because they search actively and attend differentially to various stimuli, newborns appear to be absorbing and storing information; yet it seems unlikely that they perceive the world as adults do. Perception involves the organization and interpretation of simple sense impressions, and mature perception depends on neurological development, experience, and learning.

It now appears that a number of rather complex perceptual abilities traditionally thought to be products of learning are probably innate. Take, for example, the perception of solidity. Earlier writings suggested that the ability to identify objects as solid is the result of learning to associate visual cues with tactile impressions. Some ingenious recent research suggests that this is not the case, however. By placing polarizing goggles over infants' eyes and using polarizing filters and rear-projection screens, the experimenter created an optical illusion—a cube appearing in front of a screen looking very real and solid. It was, however, intangible; when the infants attempted to grasp it they felt only empty air. Every one of the infant subjects in the experiment, ranging in age from 12 to 24 weeks, showed marked surprise (crying and startled responses) when they reached for the cube and felt nothing. The younger infants simply cried and their facial expressions changed; the older ones reacted more strongly, staring at their hands and appearing very startled. These infants showed no signs of surprise when they felt real objects suspended before them. The investigator interpreted the infants' surprise when they reached for the illusory object as evidence thay they "expected" an object to be solid and touchable. If this expectation depends on learning to coordinate vision and touch, this learning must take place before the age of 12 weeks.

To rule out the possibility that the infants' surprise was due to very early learning, the investigator began to work with even younger infants, 2-week-olds. At this age, babies ordinarily show a defensive response when a solid object approaches them. They pull their heads back or put their hands between their face and the object, as though to shield themselves. These responses are accompanied by distress and crying—often very vigorous crying. Again using projectors and goggles, the investigator moved an illusory object toward the neonate's face. All the infants tested exhibited defensive reactions. The investigator therefore concluded that there is a built-in association between visual objects and the expectation that they are solid and can be touched.

Consider another complex kind of perception, the perception of depth. Many species of animals are born with the ability to perceive depth—and thus to avoid falling into crevices—and depth perception is apparently present in humans very early. In one experiment, babies a few months of age were placed, individually, in the center of a heavy solid glass rectangle. Extending from the center on one side was a checkerboard pattern, placed directly beneath the glass. On the other side, the same kind of pattern was placed several feet below the glass, thus giving the illusion of depth or a visual cliff. If the infant's mother came to the "shallow" end of the table and called to her child, the infant would readily crawl to her. If the mother called from the "deep" side, however, the infant would not cross the cliff or approach her, *even though the infant could pat the glass and knew that the surface was solid.* This suggests that the ability to perceive depth is innate.

While attention to movement and to contrast are clearly unlearned responses, experience very soon begins to play a role in attention. If you show 1- or 2-week-old newborns a black and white outline of a human face and a meaningless design, they look equally long at each of them, for both stimuli contain strong contrasts. However, 4-month-old infants show much longer fixations (greater attention) to outlines of faces than they do to meaningless designs. By this age, infants' attention has become more selective; they are attracted more to familiar and meaningful stimuli than to meaningless ones.

Learning and Memory in Neonates and Infants

Infants are capable of learning from the very first few days of life. Newborns can be conditioned to turn their heads to one side in response to the sound of a bell coming from that direction. During conditioning trials in one experiment, each time a bell was sounded to the left side of newborns' heads and they responded by turning their heads in that direction, they received a nipple to suck on and milk. If they did not turn their heads during the first few trials, the nipple was brushed lightly against the lower left corner of their mouths to elicit head turning, a reflex response to this stimulation.

In each experimental session, the sound of a bell was paired with the nipple ten times. During the first sessions, the infants sometimes turned their heads to the left when the bell sounded and sometimes they did not. After 17 or 18 such experimental sessions—a total of about 175 trials—infants as young as 3 days learned to turn their heads toward the nipple every time they heard the bell. Of course this kind of conditioning can be achieved much more rapidly in older infants. Three-month-old babies become conditioned in about one-fourth of the number of trials (about 40) that it takes to condition a 3-day-old.

Very early in life, experience and reward begin to affect the frequency with which infants manifest "social responses" such as cooing and smiling. Recall the study in which 3-month-old babies increased the frequency of their vocalizations after they had been rewarded (smiled at and touched on the abdomen) by the investigator each time they made a sound. When the experimenter stopped rewarding the vocalizations, their frequency decreased sharply. In another study, infants were rewarded (picked up, smiled at, and talked to) every time they smiled. After this, they smiled much more frequently; but when rewards were discontinued, the frequency of smiles diminished significantly, and protests (crying, kicking, and howling) increased. These experiments demonstrate that even very young infants learn responses that lead to rewards; through rewards, adults can exert a significant degree of control over an infant's behavior.

Observational learning also begins early in life. Piaget's account of his daughter's "deferred imitation" at 16 months of age has been cited as a classic example. The little girl was visited by a little boy who threw a terrible temper tantrum, screaming, pushing, stamping his feet. She had never observed such an event before and watched in amazement. The next day she reproduced the boy's actions accurately. It may be inferred that she had stored some representation of the event (perhaps a visual image) and used it as a guide or model in her imitation.

More and more, researchers have come to believe that, for the most part, the infant's behavior is not controlled, shaped, and molded primarily by external forces and rewards; rather, infants *intend to learn and initiate learning*—that is, they actively participate in the learning process. There is ample evidence to support this view. For example, Jerome Bruner and his colleagues at the Center for Cognitive Studies at Harvard University discovered that infants could learn to "regulate" or "control" a reflex response such as sucking in order to produce satisfying changes in their environment.

Each of their subjects—infants 4, 5, or 6 weeks of age—was seated in a high chair in front of a panel of colored light bulbs. In the infant's mouth was placed a pacifier nipple connected to an electrical system so that if the infant sucked in long, hard bursts, colored bulbs flashed on and off, giving a "light show." Infants learned immediately, during the very first experimental session, to suck in ways that produced this desirable show. If conditions were reversed so that hard sucking turned off the lights, they quickly learned to desist from sucking this way. The infants' learning was so rapid that it cannot be explained simply as the result of rewards. Rather, the investigators conclude that there is some kind of inherent predisposition—a kind of built-in program of action in the infant's mind—that permits babies to pick up rules quickly and to establish cause-and-effect relationships between what they do and what they perceive. The investigators believe that conditioning requires a great deal of time because infants are adverse to such learning; when infants use their own initiatives, fulfill their own intentions, and are active in the process, they learn very quickly.

It has been suggested that, like older children, infants find it rewarding to do things on their own initiative and to exercise some control over the environment. Eight-week-old infants participated in an experiment in which they rapidly learned to move their heads frequently when they found that their movements produced an interesting "show," the rotation of a brightly painted mobile hanging over the crib. The infants' heads rested on a "pressure sensing" pillow that had an electronic connection with the mobiles, so that they could control the rotation of the mobile simply by moving their heads slightly. A control group of infants of the same age also saw a rotating mobile, but they could not control its movements.

The infants who were able to control the rotation of the mobile soon learned to do so and moved their heads frequently, the number of head movements increasing continuously for the 14 days of the experiment. In contrast, the controls showed no change in the frequency of head movements during the same period. Apparently the infants readily "caught on" to the fact that the interesting movements of the mobile were contingent on their actions, and they were interested in controlling them. It was noted also that the experimental group enjoyed the experience of controlling the mobiles; they gazed at the mobiles attentively, often smiling and cooing as they watched.

Using conditioning techniques, one prominent European researcher, Hanus Papousek, "taught" infants 2 and 3 months old to make fairly intricate responses. For example, some of the infants learned to turn their heads to the right to receive milk when a bell sounded and to turn their heads to the left to receive milk when they heard a buzzer. Four-month-old infants could be conditioned to respond to a bell by making two turns to one side and then two to the other or to alternate between turning their heads to the right and to the left. But Papousek does not believe that the infants were simply molded or shaped by rewards to perform these complex responses. Rather, his observations of the infants as they were being conditioned led him to conclude that they *intend* to learn; the conditioning experiences simply serve as incentives to devise strategies and to solve problems, to experiment, and to seek correct solutions. For example, he noted that the infants frequently seemed to correct themselves spontaneously as soon as they found they did not receive milk on the side to which they had turned; they also acted as if they expected the milk when they made the correct response.

MEMORY   Infants develop the capacity to remember an event that occurred earlier—that is, to store experience—when they are between 2 and 3 months of age. Evidence of this is found in a study in which 10-week-old infants were repeatedly shown a picture of a face projected on a screen in front of them for one second. After 10 or 15 trials, they stopped responding to the stimulus, became bored, and looked away; they had become *habituated* to this stimulus. Then the stimulus changed; a checkerboard was substituted for the face. The change captured the children's attention, and they looked at the new stimulus intently for a few seconds. Increased attention to the new stimulus after habituation to an old one is called *dishabituation*. Habituation and dishabituation are evidence that infants have some ability to remember events. Infants cannot respond to a stimulus as "familiar" or "different" unless they have some sort of memory for earlier events.

Ten-week-old infants can remember an event for 24 hours. One group of infants this age were shown an orange ball bouncing up and down on a platform for a few minutes. Twenty-four hours later they were shown the same stimulus again. This time they responded less and became bored with it (that is, they habituated) more rapidly than did infants seeing the stimulus for the first time. Apparently the event of the previous day was recognized as familiar; that is, the infants remembered it.

Piaget on Infancy

The recent emphasis on the infant's cognitive processes and active participation in the learning process is attributable, in large part, to the enormous influence of the theories of Jean Piaget of the University of Geneva, the most eminent developmental psychologist of the twentieth century. Piaget is an acute observer of children, and he uses both naturalistic observation and informal experimental techniques in his research. The subjects of his earliest observations were his own children, but he subsequently greatly expanded the population he observed.

For Piaget, intelligence is the ability to adapt to the environment and to new situations—to think and act in adaptive ways. Furthermore, in his view, children always play an active and creative part in their own cognitive development. As we shall see in chapter 3, cognitive development proceeds in a regular, invariant sequence of stages; that is, every child goes through the same succession of stages of development. The sequence is neither biologically determined nor the direct result of experience. Instead, cognitive development is the outcome of a continuous interaction between the *structure* of the organism and the environment. At each stage, the child has certain mental capabilities and certain organizing tendencies, and these influence the ways in which the child interacts with or "operates on" the environment and his or her experiences. Experience is a necessary element in cognitive development, but experience does not direct or shape development; the child actively selects, orders, organizes, and interprets his or her experiences.

According to Piaget's theory, the first stage of cognitive development—the one with which we are concerned here—is the *sensorimotor period* extending from birth to about 18 months or 2 years of age. During this time, children's perceptions improve and they perform increasingly complex actions, but they do not have mental representations or thought processes that depend on symbolic language. The infant's intelligence progresses from simple reflexes and vague awareness of the environment to more distinct, complex, and precise perceptions and increasingly more systematic and well-organized responses.

The *sensorimotor* period is divided into six phases. For the first month, infants actively exercise the reflexes present at birth (the only mental "structures" at this time); as a result, these become modified, elaborated, and more efficient. The second phase, which lasts from roughly 1 to 4 months, involves *coordination of reflexes and responses*. Hand movements become coordinated with eye movements; what is heard is looked at (orienting reflex); children reach for objects, grasp them, and suck them. If by chance one action produces an enjoyable result, the infant immediately attempts to repeat this action. For example, if he finds that sucking his hand is enjoyable, he begins to make active efforts to insert his hand into his mouth.

In the third phase, approximately 4 to 8 months, infants begin to crawl and to manipulate objects. They show interest in the environment and begin to anticipate the consequences of their actions, *intentionally* repeating actions that produce interesting and enjoyable results. For example, at 4 months of age a baby kicks her legs in order to swing a toy suspended over her crib. Moreover, since she is now interested in the objective world, she begins to look for objects she has lost sight of.

In the fourth phase, the child begins to differentiate means from ends and uses previously learned responses to attain goals. Thus, if a desirable toy is hidden from an infant's view, she will actively search for it and will remove an obstacle in order to get it.

The fifth phase, beginning at 11 or 12 months of age, is characterized by active experimentation, novelty-seeking exploration, variation, and modification of behavior. Children appear to be genuinely interested in novelty and manifest a great deal of curiosity. They experiment a great deal, dropping objects just to watch them fall, pulling toys toward them with strings, and using sticks to push things around. Their activities become more deliberate, constructive, and original.

Between 18 months and 2 years of age the child is in the sixth and final phase of the sensorimotor period, one that represents a very important cognitive advance. In this phase we see the real beginnings of the capacity to respond to or think about objects and events that are not immediately observable. Children begin to *invent* new means of accomplishing goals through "mental combinations"—that is, through imagination and ideas. They "think out" a problem before attempting to solve it, and they use ideas and images to invent new ways of accomplishing goals. Objects may be considered in new relationships to one another. Thus, a child may use a stick as a tool for drawing an object toward him even though he has never used a stick in this way previously. Problem solving, remembering, planning, imagining, and pretending are all possible at this stage.

Obviously, infants make tremendous cognitive progress between birth and 2 years of age. Their development is gradual and continuous rather than abrupt and sudden. Starting from an undifferentiated state in which they hardly distinguish themselves from the environment and can react only in reflex ways, they move to a level of genuine intelligence—to a stage in which they can represent objects mentally, solve problems, and invent new ways of doing things.

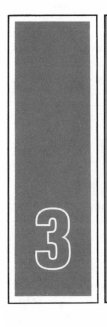

Language,
Cognitive Development,
and Intelligence

For normal children, infancy ends with the beginnings of real language. As we noted, in Piaget's theory the first period of cognitive development, the sensorimotor, is completed when children begin to use images and symbols, including language, in their thinking. We shall return to Piaget's theory of cognitive development after infancy shortly; first, we shall take a closer look at language acquisition and its influence on cognition.

It would be difficult to overestimate the importance of language in a child's development. A major part of the child's learning—at home, in the neighborhood, in school, and from the mass media—depends on language, the basis of all social communication. The functioning of the social structure and the transmission of culture from one generation to the next depend largely on language.

As adults, we use language in most of our cognitive functions—in thinking, abstraction, concept formation, planning, reasoning, remembering, judging, and problem solving. This does not necessarily mean, however, that language is *required* for cognitive functions, although some theorists have argued that this is the case. The relationship between language and thought is a very complex one and is a subject of controversy. Many American and Russian psychologists maintain that the development of thought depends on language. They argue that in the course of development, the child's overt speech gradually becomes internalized, and as this occurs, internal speech is increasingly used to organize activities and regulate actions. Vygotsky, a famous Russian psychologist, claimed that children's actions are "mediated through words." Therefore, it is hardly surprising that children's cognitive abilities progress markedly as they acquire language and as their verbal facility improves. After children acquire some names or labels that are applied to objects or events, such as "dog" or "Grandma coming," they are likely to react in the same way to all stimuli that have these labels (approaching and petting four-legged animals called dogs and smiling when Grandma arrives). This is known as *verbal mediation*, or *mediated generalization*, and many have stressed the importance of such mediation in concept formation, abstraction, problem solving, thinking, and learning.

Piaget's view is in sharp contrast with this. According to Piaget, language plays only a limited, although important, role in the formation of the child's thought. He does not deny that internal speech sometimes controls behavior but holds that language does not shape thought; thought involves more than language. Thought in the form of sensorimotor intelligence begins to develop before language does, and there is evidence that infants use images in their thinking, even though they do not yet use language (see chapter 2). Furthermore, deaf children are only slightly handicapped in many intellectual and cognitive tasks, including tests of reasoning, although these children are considerably retarded in verbal ability. In brief, although language is often used in thinking, it is possible to think without using language. For these reasons, Piaget believes that thought is not completely dependent on language.

John Flavell, a leading researcher and scholar in the area of cognition, presents the Piagetian point of view:

> There is reason to think that linguistic development is, in good part, a matter of learning how *what you already know* is expressed in your native language. ... For example, 12–24 month olds can intelligently group (categorize) and order objects manually on the basis of various functional and physical relationships that hold among the objects, even though they may not yet be able to name most of these categories and relationships. ... The young child's months of sensorimotor activity have provided him with a great deal of this kind of uncoded knowledge about how objects can be related to one another, and it now remains to map all this knowledge into a linguistic system, so that he can tell himself and others what he knows implicitly. Piaget and a number of other psychologists take the position, then, that language development largely follows on the heels of general cognitive development, not the other way around.*

* J. Flavell, *Cognitive Development* (Englewood Cliffs, N.J.: Prentice-Hall, Inc., 1977), p. 38.

Once acquired, however, language becomes the most important of our symbolic systems and undoubtedly facilitates thinking, reasoning, concept formation, learning, and remembering. Soon after they have acquired language, young children use words in trying to solve problems, often talking to themselves, thinking out loud and guiding their actions with their speech: "I'll find a stick . . . then I'll push that box out of the way. . . ."

Verbal labeling and rehearsing are often effective in facilitating memory, although children can remember scenes and objects that they cannot label accurately. Complex problems are more readily solved if verbal mediators are used to label component parts and to guide actions. This was dramatically illustrated in a Russian study in which children were shown pictures of butterfly wings and instructed to match these with similar ones in a large array. The matchings were to be made on the basis of patterns of wing markings, a difficult task because the pattern cannot be readily or easily separated from the color. An experimental group was taught labels (words for spots and stripes) to describe various patterns. These children were able to make the matchings much more accurately than a control group of children who were not given any descriptive words. Attaching labels (verbal mediators) gave the patterns some distinctiveness that made the matching task easier.

LANGUAGE DEVELOPMENT

Since the late 1950s the field of psycholinguistics—the psychological study of language and its development—has become very prominent and productive. Large samples of children's vocalizations and speech have been recorded and minutely analyzed, but the process of language acquisition is not yet fully understood. Clearly, children's experiences have powerful impacts on their language acquisition; babies learn to speak the language they hear others around them speaking. Children cannot acquire labels or concepts of things that are not part of the culture in which they grow up. If wigwams or igloos are unknown in their culture, they cannot form concepts of these things. An American child acquires only one label for rice; an Indonesian child has labels for many types of rice and differentiates among these: rice in the paddies, mature but unharvested rice, boiled rice, and so forth.

Psycholinguists offer impressive arguments that biological factors—structures "built into" the human organism—also loom large in language development. The development of phonemes, the most elementary speech sounds, follows an unvaried sequence that strongly suggests a maturational basis. Sounds formed at the back of the mouth, such as h, ordinarily appear first and decrease in relative frequency as sounds involving the use of the teeth and lips become more common. Children of all nations and cultures make the same sounds and in the same order. English and American infants pronounce French nasals and French gutteral r's as well as German vowel sounds, and deaf babies utter the same phonemes—and at about the same time—as children who hear normally. All babies coo and babble, repeating the same sound over again (for example, "da da da da") from about the third month until the end of the first year, and imitation of adult speech generally begins at about 9 months of age. New sounds are not learned by imitation, however; babies imitate only those sounds that they have already uttered spontaneously.

The most impressive evidence that "built-in," inherent capacities are of overriding importance in language acquisition is the amazingly rapid development of the child's comprehension and use of language, particularly the child's early mastery of grammar. Even casual observation attests to the fact that comprehension of language generally precedes linguistic performance. A baby at about 10 months of age responds to simple commands but does not utter a real word until a few months later. When requested, babies between 10 and 14 months of age have little difficulty finding common objects such as spoons, hats, and toy cars, even though they do not yet use the words for these objects in their own speech. In addition, children this age understand some complex word combinations. One 15-month-old child in a developmental study produced only two words, one for dog and other animals (di) and one for refusing requests (uh-uh), but correctly carried out the investigator's requests to "show me the baby's (his sister's) bottle" and "give me your bottle." Although the child could produce relatively little language, he already had the cognitive skills that enabled him to make the distinctions between give and show, your and the baby's, and he had stored some knowledge of how combinations of words are interpreted.

Children generally speak their first word at approximately 12 months of age. This is usually a single or duplicated syllable such as da-da or ma-ma, referring to some highly salient person, animal, or object. The word may function as a whole sentence; "da-da" may mean "Where is Daddy," "I see Daddy," or, accompanied by a pointing gesture toward a shoe on the floor, "That's Daddy's shoe." At about 18 months of age, babies in all cultures begin to put words together in simple primitive sentences ("see shoe," "where doggie," "more milk," "bye-bye car"). These early sentences are essentially abbreviated, or telegraphic, versions of adult sentences, made up primarily of nouns and verbs with a few adjectives. They do not ordinarily include prepositions such as *in, on,* or *under,* articles such as *a* or *the,* auxiliary verbs such as *have* or *did,* or the verbs *am, is,* or *are.* After a few months of producing these simple two-word sentences, the child begins to put longer strings of words together in sentences. And by the time they are 3 or 4 years old, children speak sentences that reveal their mastery of the complex structure of their own language. In the short span of 2 or 2½ years, children achieve an almost adult way of speaking. It is estimated that, by the time they are 6, American children have vocabularies of between 8,000 and 14,000 words. This means that they have added an average of five to eight words a day between the ages of 1 and 6!

Most importantly, very young children continually produce new sentences—generate utterances they have never heard before— and these sentences conform to the grammatical rules of the child's own language, some of which are very complex. The speech of 3- or 4-year-olds reveals that they have acquired substantial knowledge of important grammatical rules governing word order, the formation of plurals, and past and future tenses. A pointed demonstration of the young child's mastery of abstract and general rules of a language has been provided by Slobin, who analyzed the following simple interchange between a mother and a 3-year-old:

Mother: Where did you go with Grandpa?
Child: We goed in the park.

The child's answer shows that she understood all the major elements of the mother's question: it asked about directed motion, to a goal, involving the listener and a participant, and in the past. The answer also reflects the child's knowledge of the rules of sentence construction, so that she can generate an appropriate sentence of her own. For example, the use of *we* responds to the mother's use of *you.* The word *goed,* although an error from an adult point of view, reveals that she has acquired the rules for forming past tense by adding *ed;* she has simply overgeneralized this rule and treated an irregular word as though it were a regular one. The phrase "in the park" shows that the child has only partial mastery of the English rules for talking about the goals of directed motion.

This mastery of highly abstract and general rules is a formidable accomplishment for a young child, and it is made very rapidly. Such accomplishments, which are universal, would probably not be possible unless there were some innate, biological capability for language acquisition—unless "the child comes to the task prepared, in some way, to process ... [linguistic] data ... and to form the kinds of structure which are characteristic of human language."* Many psycholinguists, therefore, have concluded that the child is "creatively constructing language on his own in accordance with *innate and intrinsic* capacities.... developing new theories of the structure, modifying and discarding old theories as he goes [italics ours]."†

Most research in psycholinguistics has focused on the acquisition of grammar and syntax, but there is mounting interest in problems of semantics, of what the child's speech *means*. The same simple combination of two words may have many different meanings that must be inferred from the contexts in which the sentences are produced. Thus "baby hat" used in different contexts can mean "That is the baby's hat" (pointing to a hat) or "Mommie is putting on my hat." The child intends to convey a range of meanings, but he cannot yet express these different meanings.

Interestingly, it appears that regardless of the culture in which they live and the language they hear around them, all babies express the same thoughts in their first sentences—thoughts reflecting the interests and capabilities of the sensorimotor stage of development. Analyses of the first sentences of English, German, Russian, Finnish, Turkish, Samoan, and Kenyan children reveal that

> there is a striking uniformity across children and across languages in the kinds of meaning expressed in simple two-word utterances, suggesting that semantic development is closely tied to general cognitive development. The following range of semantic relations is typical of early child speech:
>
> | | |
> |---|---|
> | IDENTIFICATION: | *see doggie* |
> | LOCATION: | *book there* |
> | REPETITION: | *more milk* |
> | NONEXISTENCE: | *allgone thing* |
> | NEGATION: | *not wolf* |
> | POSSESSION: | *my candy* |
> | ATTRIBUTION: | *big car* |
> | AGENT-ACTION: | *mama walk* |
> | ACTION-OBJECT: | *hit you* |
> | AGENT-OBJECT: | *mama book* |
> | ACTION-LOCATION: | *sit chair* |

* D. I. Slobin, *Psycholinguistics*, 2nd ed. (Glenview, Ill.: Scott, Foresman & Company), in press.
† Ibid.

ACTION-RECIPIENT: *give paper*
ACTION-INSTRUMENT: *cut knife*
QUESTION: *where ball?*

The universality of such a list is impressive.*

THE CHILD'S THOUGHT

Preoperational Thought

As the child's language becomes more complex, new cognitive processes appear and intellectual skills increase. The second broad period of intellectual development according to Piaget is the *pre-operational*, extending from approximately 1½ to 7 years of age. Recall that at the end of the first period of cognitive development, the sensorimotor, the child manipulates objects and uses them as a means of attaining goals. All of the child's thinking and reasoning is, however, limited to objects and events that are immediately present and directly perceived. In contrast, in the preoperational period, the child begins to use *mental symbols*—images or words—that stand for or *represent* objects that are not present. Simple examples are found in the child's play: a bicycle may be an airplane, a box becomes a house, and a piece of cloth is used as a robe. The use of symbols is also seen in *deferred imitation*, that is, imitation of a model that is no longer present. The following example of deferred imitation is taken from one of Piaget's observations of his daughter, when she was 16 months old.

> [Jacqueline] had a visit from a little boy [of eighteen months] whom she used to see from time to time, and who, in the course of the afternoon, got into a terrible temper. He screamed as he tried to get out of a play-pen and pushed it backward, stamping his feet. J. stood watching him in amazement, never having witnessed such a scene before. The next day, she herself screamed in her play-pen and tried to move it, stamping her foot lightly several times in succession.†

Since the model was not present at the time she copied his

---

* D. I. Slobin, "Seven Questions About Language Development," in *Psychology, 1972*, ed. P. C. Dodwell (London: Penguin, 1972).

† J. Piaget, *Play, Dreams and Imitation in Childhood* (New York: W. W. Norton & Co., 1962), p. 63.

behavior, it may be inferred that Jacqueline had a mental representation of the tantrum and then based her behavior on this. Because she was able to symbolize the boy's action in this way, she could copy his behavior at a later time.

Piaget does not believe that the child's earliest use of words, during the sensorimotor period, is symbolic; rather, during this period words are concrete, intimately related to the child's ongoing activities or desires. During the preoperational period, however, the child gradually begins to use words to stand for absent objects and events. When she was 23 months old, Jacqueline returned from a trip and reported to her father that "Robert cry, ducks swim in lake, gone away." She was able to use words to stand for these past events.

During the early part of the preoperational stage, between the ages of approximately 2 and 4, children are egocentric, that is, centered about themselves. They are unable to take another person's point of view. This is clearly seen in children's speech and communication: they make little real effort to adapt what they say to the needs of the listener. Children's thoughts, too, are egocentric. As they see it, the sun, moon, and clouds follow them around.

Children between 2 and 4 have no real conception of abstract principles that guide classification. If you present young children with a group of geometric shapes (for example, squares, circles, triangles, and stars) and ask them to "put together things that are alike," they do not use overall guiding principles in doing the task. Sometimes similarities determine what is put together; at other times, they group things on what appears to be a random basis—blue circles and yellow triangles or a red square and two blue circles. Children between the ages of 5 and 7 produce real classes of objects, grouping them together on the basis of size, shape, or color. Yet even at this age children cannot deal with what Piaget calls *class inclusion*: they cannot reason simultaneously about the whole and a part of the whole. For example, if you show a 5-year-old ten red roses and five yellow roses and ask her whether there are more red roses or more roses, she is likely to reply that there are more red roses. When she deals with a subclass, the larger class is destroyed; she cannot conceive that a flower can belong to two classes at the same time.

Nor is the preoperational child able to handle problems of *ordering*, or, as Piaget calls it, *seriating*. In one of Piaget's studies, children were given 10 sticks that differed only in size. They were asked to select the smallest stick. After this they were told, "Now try to put first the smallest, then one a bit bigger, than another a little bit bigger, and so on." Four-year-old children did not solve this problem successfully. Some of them made random arrangements; others ordered a few sticks but not all of them.

The concepts of preoperational children and their understanding of situations are likely to be determined by their immediate perceptions, and they often perceive only a single salient aspect of a particular object or event. Ordinarily they will not relate different aspects or dimensions of a situation to one another. For example, in one experiment a child is given two equal balls of clay and asked to roll one of them into a long sausage, or to flatten it into a pancake, or to break it into small pieces. Then the child is asked whether the quantity of clay has increased, decreased, or remains equal. Most 5- and 6-year-olds think that a change in form necessarily produces a change in amount. Being able to take account of only one dimension (such as length) at a time, a child of this age is likely to report that the sausage contains more clay than the ball because it is longer.

Or in a parallel situation, a child is presented with two identical glasses, each of them containing the same amount of juice (fig. 3.1). After he or she agrees that each of the glasses contains the same amount of juice, the liquid is poured from one glass into a third, shorter, wider glass. The column of liquid in the third glass is therefore shorter and wider than that in the other glass. The child is now asked whether the two glasses contain equal amounts. The preoperational child is likely to judge that the amount of liquid changes with the change in its appearance—for example, that there is more juice in the taller, thinner glass because the level of the liquid is higher in that glass. Children at this stage do not yet realize that as the level of the liquid changes, there is a corresponding change in the width, which compensates for the change in level.

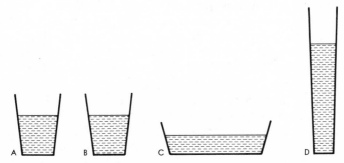

Fig. 3.1 Conservation of continuous quantities.

The Period of Concrete Operations

The next broad period in cognitive development, *concrete operations*, begins at about 7 years of age. During this period the deficiencies of the preoperational period are, to a large extent, overcome. Children acquire the concept of *conservation*, or what Piaget labels the *principle of invariance*. Faced with the questions about the amount of clay in the ball or suasage, or the amount of liquid in the glasses, they understand that the amounts do not change just because the shape changes. They are likely to reason that "if you make the sausage into a ball again you see that nothing is added and nothing is taken away," or speaking of the liquid they may say that "what it gained in height it lost in width."

Furthermore, they acquire the concept of *reversibility*—the idea that, in thought, steps can be retraced, actions can be canceled, and the original situation can be restored. Thus, in making a sausage of a ball of clay, the diminution in the height of the ball is compensated for by the increase in length, so that the same quantity of clay is maintained. The number 2 can be squared to get 4, and extracting the square root of 4 yields 2. Using the concept of reversibility, children can interrupt a sequence of steps in problem solving if they see that they are not succeeding, and they can then return mentally to the beginning and start again.

Operational children succeed in other tasks where preoperational children fail. They have more advanced notions of classes in an abstract sense and can sort objects on the basis of such characteristics as shape, color, and size. They also understand *relationships*; for example, they recognize that an object can belong to both classes and subclasses simultaneously (white flowers are a subclass of flowers, and a bouquet has more flowers than white flowers). While preoperational children think in absolute terms—light or dark, big or small—and do not seem to understand relational terms, children in the period of concrete operations think in terms of longer, higher, wider. They realize that a brother must be the brother of someone, an object must be bigger or smaller—or to the right or left—compared with something else. When given a set of sticks, the operational child can easily arrange them in order of size. The child's overall plan or strategy in classifying and seriating shows an understanding of the *relationships* among things observed.

The cognitive achievements of the stage of concrete operations make children's thought at this period much more solid and flexible than it was earlier. They are capable of elementary logical processes—or what Piaget calls *operations*—reasoning deductively, from premise to conclusion, in a logical way. But they do so only in limited and elementary ways, applying logic only to concrete events, perceptions, and representations of these. They do not think in abstract terms or reason about verbal or hypothetical propositions. Thus, while 8-, 9-, or 10-year-olds have no trouble in ordering a series of dolls or sticks according to height, they have difficulty with verbal problems such as "Edith is taller than Susan; Edith is shorter than Lilly; who is the tallest of the three?"

Memory

A child's capacity to remember—to store information and retrieve it later on—also improves with age, particularly during the period of concrete operations. Memory is commonly tested by reading a series of numbers or nonsense syllables (KIB, NOL) and instructing the subject to repeat them or by showing a series of pictures and asking the child to recall or recognize them a few minutes later (short-term memory) or after a longer period (long-term memory). Four-year-olds can recall three of four numbers immediately after hearing them, while 12-year-olds recall six or seven.

The reasons for age differences in ability to remember are not entirely clear, but some data suggest that older children have learned to use certain strategies in storing information, while younger children have not yet acquired these strategies. For example, *rehearsing* a list of words or objects (repeating them to oneself) during the interval between presentation and the time that memory is tested results in improved memory for these stimuli. Older children are likely to rehearse in this way spontaneously, but younger ones do not. To illustrate, in one experiment children of ages 5, 7, and 10 were shown pictures of seven objects, and an experimenter slowly pointed to three of them. The children had been instructed that they would later be asked to point to the same pictures in the same order that the experimenter did. An investigator who could read lips observed the children closely and found that spontaneous rehearsal of the order increased with age: very few 5-year-olds, a little more than half of the 7-year-olds, and almost all the 10-year-olds rehearsed the order. Subsequently, 6-year-olds participated in an experiment using the same procedures. Some of them rehearsed the order of pictures spontaneously, while others did not. The "spontaneous rehearsers" recalled the sequences better than those who did not rehearse. The nonrehearsers were then trained to rehearse, and when they did so, their recall increased to the level of the spontaneous rehearsers.

Organization of the material to be remembered (for example, grouping or clustering the stimulus words in categories such as animals or kitchen utensils) and creating mental images or finding some ways of associating two or more things to be remembered (for example, finding some common feature among them) are also effective strategies for enhancing recall. Older children are more likely than younger ones to use these strategies deliberately and spontaneously. Age differences in capacity to remember may be attributable largely to differences in the inclination to use these strategies.

Formal Operations

Dealing with verbal expressions of logical relationships requires "formal operations"—as distinct from "concrete operations"—and children do not ordinarily use these until the age of 11 or 12. In the view of Piaget and Inhelder (his chief collaborator), the application of logical rules and reasoning to abstract problems and propositions is the essence of mature intellectual ability. This final stage of intellectual development, the stage of formal operations, begins early in adolescence. The adolescent can reason deductively, making hypotheses about problem solutions and holding many variables in mind simultaneously. He or she is capable of scientific reasoning and of formal logic, and can follow the *form* of an argument while disregarding its concrete content—hence the term *formal operations*.

In contrast with operational children who are concerned only with concrete objects, perceptions, and representations of these, adolescents seem preoccupied with thinking. They take their own thoughts as an object and think about thinking, evaluating their own and others' logic, ideas, and thoughts. They consider general laws as well as real situations, and they are concerned with the hypothetically possible as well as with reality. Their dependence on the perception or manipulation of concrete objects is greatly reduced; they need no longer confine their attentions to the immediate situation. By the time they are 15, adolescents solve problems by analyzing them logically and formulating hypotheses about *possible* outcomes, about what *might* occur. The hypotheses may be complex ones involving many possible combinations of outcomes. Nevertheless, the individual who has attained the stage of formal operations attempts to test hypotheses either mentally or in reality by experiments.

The adolescent's ability to think scientifically is clearly illustrated by one experiment reported by Inhelder and Piaget. A subject is presented with five bottles of colorless liquid. The contents of bottles 1, 3, and 5, when combined, produce a brownish color; the fourth contains a color-reducing solution; and the second is neutral. The problem is to produce the brown solution. Adolescents in the stage of formal operations discover the solution little by little, by combining the various possibilities logically and determining the effectiveness or neutrality of each liquid.

THE DEVELOPMENT OF INTELLIGENCE

The discussion of Piaget's work in the preceding section focused on *qualitative* descriptions of the changes that occur as the child's cognitive abilities mature. In this approach, mental growth is viewed as a series of stages, a succession of new mental organizations or structures that are the foundations for the emergence of new mental abilities.

American psychologists have traditionally taken another, more quantitative, approach to the problem of mental growth. This is the *mental test* or *psychometric approach*, which stresses *individual differences* in intelligence and the factors underlying these differences. Intelligence is defined in terms of scores on a test, and intellectual growth is measured by the child's increasing ability to pass more items—and more difficult items—on an intelligence test as he or she grows older. There is little emphasis on the processes or the components of mental ability underlying changes in general ability.

Scores on intelligence tests are usually expressed in terms of an intelligence quotient, or IQ, defined as the ratio between *mental age* (MA), which is a score based on performance on an intelligence test, and *chronological age*, multiplied by 100 (IQ = MA/CA × 100). For example, if a 7-year-old has a mental age of 7, the IQ is 100 (average for the population at large). If he or she has a mental age of 6, the IQ is 85, which is generally considered in the "low average" range, falling in the lower 25 percent of the population. With a mental age of 10, the IQ is 10/7 × 100, or 143, in the "very superior" range, the top 1 percent of the population. Only 3 percent of the population fall below IQ 70, the upper limit of the range of mental deficiency.

IQ scores have been used very widely in clinical evaluations, in educational counseling, and in school placement, because the score tells immediately where individuals rank in brightness compared with others their own age. The use of intelligence tests with their emphasis on individual differences has recently raised a number of important social questions and become a source of major conflicts, however. One critical problem has to do with the use of intelligence tests with children from severely deprived, poverty backgrounds. Related to this are the issues of the hereditary determinants of intelligence, race and socioeconomic differences in intellectual test performance, and the stability of the IQ over time (from early childhood to adolescence, for example). These are the issues to which we now turn.

The Nature of the Intelligence Test

In defining intelligence, most testers—and psychologists who have constructed intelligence tests—stress the ability to think in abstract terms and to reason, together with the ability to use these functions for *adaptive purposes*. Piaget regards intelligence as a specific instance of *adaptive* behavior, of coping with the environment and organizing (and reorganizing) thought and action. All tests of intelligence contain items that tap the kinds of functions with which Piaget is concerned—problem solving, reasoning, abstract thinking. Almost all useful, valid intelligence tests are highly correlated with, and probably depend on, facility in language; all aspects of language ability tend to be positively correlated with scores in intelligence tests.

INFANT INTELLIGENCE TESTS   Because infants' language abilities and intellectual competence are not well developed in the earliest years, it is difficult to assess their intelligence. Yet, for many reasons, it is highly useful to have such evaluations. Many parents are anxious to be assured that their babies are normal. If mental retardation or neurological deficiency can be diagnosed early, more effective counseling and guidance can be given parents. Valid early assessments of intelligence would also be of tremendous value in assigning orphan children to adoptive parents or in placing them in foster homes. Consequently, a number of infant tests have been developed. The most prominent and widely used of these tests, which consist primarily of perceptual and sensorimotor items, is the Bayley Scales of Infant Development, developed after many years of intensive research. Table 3.1 lists some items from that test together with the age placements of these items (the average age at which babies can perform the task).

Unfortunately, such tests have only limited value. They may be useful in helping to diagnose gross mental deficiency, neurological defect, and specific disabilities in social responsiveness, vision, language, and hearing in young children, but they cannot predict a child's later intelligence. Scores on these so-called intelligence tests given before 18 months are absolutely worthless for the prediction of children's intellectual abilities when they are of school age.

Table 3.1

Examples of Infant Intelligence Test Items from Bayley's Scales of Infant Development

ITEM	AGE PLACEMENT (MONTHS)
Responds to voice	0.7
Visually recognizes mother	2.0
Turns head to sound of rattle	3.9
Lifts cup with handle	5.8
Responds to verbal request (e.g., to wave bye-bye)	9.1
Imitates words	12.5
Uses gestures to make wants known	14.6
Imitates crayon stroke	17.8
Follows directions in pointing to parts of a doll	19.5
Uses two-word sentence	20.6
Points to three pictures	21.9
Names three objects shown to him	24.0

Why is there so little correlation between the abilities measured by these infant tests and later intelligence? Most significantly, vastly different kinds of abilities are tapped at different ages. As a child's language becomes more highly developed and as his or her cognitive abilities improve, items involving these functions predominate in the tests, replacing the sensorimotor items of the infant scales. Items at the 2- and 3-year levels require more verbal ability and comprehension than the earlier tests, which test motor and sensory abilities almost exclusively.

In the Stanford-Binet intelligence test, a widely used test for children, items are arranged according to the age levels at which the average child can pass them. Succeeding age levels throughout the preschool and school period include increased numbers of verbal items and more problem solving, reasoning, and abstract problems. To illustrate, the 2-year-level items of this test include identifying common objects by their use, identifying major body parts, repeating two spoken digits, and placing simple blocks in a formboard. Among the 4-year-level items are naming pictures of a variety of common objects, recalling nine- and ten-word sentences, and correctly completing analogies (for instance, "In daytime it is light; at night it is _____."). Completing a drawing of a man, copying a square, defining simple words, and counting four objects are 5-year-level tasks. The 8-year-old tests involve comprehending and answering questions about a short story, recognizing absurdities in stories, defining sim-

43

ilarities and differences in pairs of objects (for example, a penny and a quarter), and general comprehension (What makes a sail boat move?). In short, as the tests show, as children grow older they can master problems of increasing difficulty, which require of them greater verbal facility, comprehension, and problem-solving ability.

IQ STABILITY AND CHANGE   While the test scores of babies under 18 months are not significantly predictive of later intelligence, IQs measured after that age tend to be more *stable*, that is, more highly correlated with scores attained in later childhood and adulthood. Table 3.2 reports correlation coefficients of intelligence test scores at various early ages with scores at ages 10 and 18 years (young adulthood) based on a longitudinal study of 252 children. As the table shows, the predictive value of the test scores increases as the child matures. IQ at age 6 or 7 is highly correlated with intelligence at ages 10 and 18. This means that, in general, the child who is superior in intelligence at age 6 remains so, while the child who is inferior at this age generally scores low at later ages.

This does *not* mean that *every* individual's standing is fixed; some children change markedly from one time to another. According to the data of one study, almost 60 percent of children change 20 or more points in IQ between the ages of 6 and 18, some improving rather consistently and some decreasing in IQ as they grow older. Such changes are, in many cases, related to personality traits and motivation, as the following case history of a subject in a longitudinal study illustrates. The boy's IQ fluctuated between 113 and 163 during his school years, the scores varying with his general state of health, psychological adjustment, and home conditions. At the age of 6, when his Stanford-Binet IQ was at its lowest, he had chronic sinus

Table 3.2

Correlations Between Intelligence Test Scores during the Preschool Years and IQ at Ages Ten and Eighteen

AGE	CORRELATION WITH IQ (STANFORD-BINET) AT AGE TEN	CORRELATION WITH IQ (WECHSLER) AT AGE EIGHTEEN
2	.37	.31
2½	.36	.24
3	.36	.35
4	.66	.42
6	.71	.61
8	.88	.70

Source: M. P. Honzik, J. W. Macfarlane, and L. Allen, "The Stability of Mental Test Performance Between Two and Eighteen Years, *Journal of Experimental Education*, 17, no. 17 (1948), 309–24.

trouble and bronchial asthma and was in bed 12 weeks. His father contracted tuberculosis, and his mother had to go to work; these changes produced a vast reorganization at home. The school reports at this time noted that the boy was restless, sensitive, and shy. In contrast, at age 10, when he scored 163, his father had recovered and was working again after a period of unemployment, his school adjustment had improved tremendously, and he was said to manifest "marvelous concentration" at school.

A systematic study of the personality correlates of IQ changes compared the 35 children in a longitudinal study who showed the greatest increase in IQ between the ages of 6 and 10 with the 35 who showed the greatest decreases during this period. In comparison with the latter, it was found, the former were more interested in school work, studied harder, and were more strongly motivated to master intellectual problems. In general, they were more oriented toward achievement, and their mothers had encouraged them since early childhood to master problems of all sorts. Apparently, intelligence-test performance to some extent reflects strength of motivation for achievement and for problem mastery. We may infer that altering this motivation may increase or decrease intelligence test scores during the school years; we shall return to this argument later.

By and large, scores on intelligence tests taken during early school years are good predictors of grammar school grades in reading, arithmetic, composition, spelling, and social studies, and they are also fairly good predictors of academic success in high school and college.

Factors Related to Performance on Intelligence Tests

Intelligence tests do not yield "pure" measures of native ability or intellectual potential; they measure and evaluate performance in specific tasks—mostly, though not entirely, of a verbal kind. This kind of performance can be influenced by many factors—in fact, by practically all the factors that help shape psychological development. Both hereditary (genetic) and environmental factors affect individual performance, but it is impossible to determine the relative proportions of an invidual's intelligence test scores that are attributable to the two sets of factors. Suppose, for example, a lower-class child, whose parents are illiterate immigrants, achieves a low score in an intelligence test. This score *may* be due to poor hereditary intellectual endowment. On the other hand, it *may* be the outcome of his impoverished background, lack of intellectual stimulation in the home, inadequate verbal ability (at least in English)—or any number of other factors or combinations of factors. We shall discuss such factors in greater detail below. Here it is important to note that knowledge of a person's score in itself tells us nothing about the reasons that he or she achieves that score.

GENETIC INFLUENCES ON INTELLIGENCE Psychologists generally accept the notion that heredity contributes to intellectual ability and probably sets the limits of this ability. But they would not agree that an individual's intelligence is genetically established at conception and is therefore fixed and unchanging. The limits that heredity sets are flexible ones.

Several kinds of evidence support the view that genetic factors contribute to the determination of intelligence as measured by test performance. In one type of study, two kinds of correlations are compared: (1) the correlation between IQ scores of children raised by their own parents and the scores of the parents, and (2) the correlation between the intelligence test scores of foster children adopted in infancy with those of their foster parents. The correlation between the IQs of parents and their natural children has generally been found to be about .50, while the correlation between the IQs of foster parents and their adopted children is, in most studies, about .20. Apparently, children resemble their true parents in intelligence-test performance to a significantly greater degree than foster children resemble foster parents. Presumably, heredity accounts for the greater correlation between true parents and their children, especially since the foster children studied were adopted very early in life.

Further impressive evidence on the role of heredity in intelligence comes from comparing correlations of the intelligence test scores of *identical* twins (who develop from a single fertilized egg and thus have exactly the same genetic constitutions) and those of fraternal twins (who develop from two fertilized eggs and hence differ genetically). The IQs of identical twins correlate very highly, about .90 on the average, while the IQs of fraternal twins correlate about .55. In other words, identical twins score very much alike on intelligence tests, and this holds true even if they were reared in quite different environments and were exposed to different experiences. In fact, the correlation between the IQs of identical twins *reared apart* was .76, while the IQs of fraternal twins who had been raised in the *same environment* correlated .55. In other words, despite being reared in vastly different environments, identical twins were more alike in tested intelligence than fraternal twins who had been raised in the same environment. Therefore, heredity must be a major determinant of intelligence, helping to set the limits within which the environment may affect a child's intelligence test score.

Nevertheless, it should be noted that even among the identical twins environmental factors had some impact on performance. The greater the differences in their environmental experiences, the more divergent were the identical twins' IQs. For example, one of a pair of identical twin girls spent a considerable part of her elementary school years in an isolated mountain setting where there were no schools. She dropped out of school entirely when very young. Her twin sister, adopted into a home where there was much emphasis on education and accomplishment, was intellectually stimulated, particularly by her foster mother. The Stanford-Binet IQ of the first girl was 92; that of the second 116, a difference of 24 points, and the latter was almost seven years more advanced than her sister in educational achievement.

ENVIRONMENTAL INFLUENCES ON INTELLIGENCE Clearly, then, environmental, personality, and motivational factors—including nutrition, intellectual stimulation, and achievement orientation in the home—also contribute significantly to intelligence. For example, anxious, fearful children have difficulty concentrating on academic and problem-solving tasks and are likely to perform poorly on intelligence tests. On the average, children of school age—particularly boys—with high scores on tests of anxiety have somewhat lower intelligence test scores than their peers who have relatively little anxiety. Children with low self-esteem who feel personally inadequate and inferior—perhaps because they are economically disadvantaged—will give up too easily in the test situation and thus perform poorly. Furthermore, children who come from deprived backgrounds probably have few role models who have used intellectual skills and education to "get ahead"; hence they are not likely to be motivated for intellectual achievement or for high-level performance on tests of cognitive functioning.

The tremendous impacts of broad, general environmental factors have been called to the psychologist's attention in rather dramatic ways through findings on social-class and race differences in intelligence test performance. Children of the upper and middle classes consistently score better than those of the lower class in intelligence tests, the average difference between the highest and the lowest social classes being about 20 IQ points. And black school children score on the average 10 to 15 points below their white schoolmates on most standard tests of intelligence. Some psychologists have interpreted these class and race differences as evidence of the hereditary determination of intelligence—that is, perhaps the upper classes and whites are of superior intellectual endowment and transmit this genetically to their children. Most psychologists, however, argue that IQ differences between racial and class groups can readily be explained in terms of environmental and experiential, rather than genetic, factors. Certainly, on the average, middle-class whites and poor blacks live in vastly different environments and have different backgrounds of experience.

Many kinds of environmental factors affect intellectual functioning. For example, inadequate nutrition during a mother's pregnancy—especially protein deficiency—can have enduring adverse effects on her child's intellectual ability. Lower-class persons are more likely than others to have inadequate diets and, consequently, to produce children of inferior intellectual ability. Some of the observed social-class and race differences in test performance may be due to such nutritional factors.

Furthermore, the contents of intelligence tests draw much more heavily on the experiences and interests of middle-class whites than of other groups. Therefore, the items of the test may be much less interesting and less meaningful to children from other social and racial groups. This, too, may help account for the apparent cognitive deficiencies of black and economically deprived children.

In addition, social-class and cultural differences in early child rearing may have highly significant impacts on intellectual functioning. Specifically, economically deprived families provide restricted experiences and little intellectual or cultural stimulation for their young children. A number of prominent psychologists have argued persuasively that intellectual interests and the motivation for intellectual competence are formed during early childhood and are very vulnerable at this period. The infant needs opportunities for learning and needs to confront various kinds of stimulation if he or she is to become intellectually motivated and alert. According to some, deprivation of cognitive and social stimulation early in life may produce irreversible adverse effects. For optimal intellectual development, the child needs to have interesting, stimulating, and pleasurable experiences, beginning in very early infancy.

Poor children, both white and black, enter school with an initial disadvantage; that is, by the time they enter school they perform more poorly on cognitive tasks and tests of intelligence, on the average, than middle-class white children. And, sadly, they frequently suffer a kind of "progressive" retardation, falling further and further behind in intellectual functioning as they go through school. Many poor children are held back in school for one year and often longer. This presents a problem of acute social importance. As a culture we are committed to drastic reduction of social, economic, and educational inequalities between social and racial groups. Can these cognitive handicaps that are manifested relatively early in life be overcome?

REDUCING THE COGNITIVE DEFICIENCIES OF ECONOMI-
CALLY DISADVANTAGED CHILDREN If early environmental stimulation can enhance subsequent intellectual performance, providing
more of this kind of stimulation and training should help overcome
cognitive deficiencies and raise the level of poor children's cognitive
functioning. In the last twenty years, there have been numerous attempts to intervene early in the child's life with special nursery school
training programs or "compensatory education." It is clear that simply
placing poor children in nursery schools and exposing them to the
usual kinds of nursery school programs do not raise the levels of
children's cognitive skills. To achieve this, intensive individual attention and training—in many cases with active participation of the
mothers—are required. This kind of early intervention *can* have significant positive results, counteracting some of the adverse effects of
early deprivation, as has been dramatically demonstrated in a study
directed by Professor Rick Heber of the University of Wisconsin.*

The participants in the study were 40 young infants and their
mothers who lived in a slum area. All the mothers had IQs of 75 or
less. Each mother-infant pair was assigned at random to either the
experimental or control group. The infants in the experimental group
were exposed to a comprehensive program of enrichment experiences, and their mothers were counseled and taught a variety of
homemaking, child rearing, and occupational skills. The control
mothers and children received no special treatment.

At 3 months of age, each experimental child was assigned to a
teacher who was in charge of him or her for seven hours a day, five
days a week, for nine months to a year. The teachers were para-
professionals who lived in the children's neighborhood and thus
shared their cultural background. Most of them were in their mid-
twenties, and their education ranged from eight grades to one year of
college. They were chosen for their jobs because they were proficient
in language, affectionate, and experienced with infants or young
children. Each teacher was responsible for total care of an infant
assigned to her, and she organized the learning environment and
carried out the educational program. This consisted largely of structured "lessons" or "experiences" designed to enhance the children's
cognitive and learning skills and, at the same time, to motivate them
to learn and to solve problems by presenting interesting and challenging tasks. After the children were 24 months of age, their daily
curriculum included activities designed to promote the development

* H. Garber and R. Heber, *The Milwaukee Project: Early Intervention as a Technique to Prevent Mental Retardation* (National Leadership Institute on Teacher
Education/Early Childhood, University of Connecticut Technical Paper, March
1973).

of language skills, reading readiness, mathematics, and problem solving. The teachers maintained continuous contact with the children's parents, reporting on progress and emphasizing accomplishments and abilities. The parents were counseled to pay attention to their children's scholastic progress and to reward cognitive achievements. At the same time, the mothers in the experimental group were instructed in homemaking and child-rearing skills, and they were given training that would prepare them for better jobs. It was assumed that the mother's improved employment potential, increased knowledge, and greater self-confidence would lead to changes in the home environment that would be beneficial to the child.

Obviously, this program was very expensive and difficult to implement, but the results were impressive and encouraging. Infant tests, administered to the experimental and control subjects several times between the ages of 6 months and 32 months, showed that the two groups performed equally well (above average, according to the norms of the test) up to the age of 14 months. By 18 months the performance of the experimental group was clearly superior, however, and the difference between the groups was even greater by 22 months. As figure 3.2 shows, the experimental and control groups diverged more and more as the children became older. (The Stan-

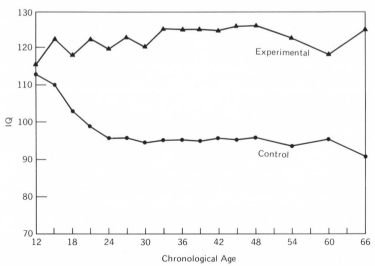

Fig. 3.2 Mean IQ performance with increasing age for the experimental and control groups. *(Adapted from H. Garber and R. Heber,* National Leadership Institute—Teacher Education/Early Childhood [*University of Connecticut Technical Paper, March 1973*].)

ford-Binet and Wechsler Intelligence Tests were given between the later ages.) At 66 months, the last time they were tested, the experimentals had an average IQ of 125; the controls' average was 91.

The investigators wanted more than one measure of cognitive development, so they also administered a number of tests of learning, problem-solving, concept formation, and language ability. The experimental children performed better than the controls on all the tests. For example, in conversations with the language tester when the children were between 18 and 30 months of age, the experimental group proved to be more verbally fluent, said more, had larger vocabularies, and produced more unusual words than did the controls. In interactions with their mothers, the experimental children supplied more information, initiated more verbal communication, and asked more questions than did the controls.

These findings are compelling evidence that the early intervention program was successful. Children's cognitive and language skills were augmented considerably. And, according to the investigators, their self-confidence was enhanced and their motivation to learn was increased. One critical question, however, is still unanswered: Will these gains be maintained in the future and be reflected in greater academic success and vocational accomplishment? Only a follow-up study of the children in the experimental and control groups can answer this question. Given such a good start, and such marked advances in cognitive performance, the children's gains from the early intervention should be lasting ones.

The compensatory intervention program we have been discussing was an unusual one in many ways. Compared with most programs, it was more comprehensive, began at an earlier age, lasted longer, and involved more individual instruction and training; also, it included work with parents as well as children. Less comprehensive compensatory nursery school programs have, in most cases, produced only modest gains in intelligence-test scores, and these have been unstable and short-lived, often disappearing within a year after the intervention program ended. For this reason, many psychologists concluded that the programs have been failures or, at best, disappointments. A recent survey of the long-range effects of ten experimental intervention programs suggests, however, that such pessimistic conclusions may have been premature. Using the data from ten follow-up studies, Professor Francis Palmer of the State University of New York at Stony Brook analyzed the elementary school records of children who had participated in nursery school intervention programs. The analysis yielded convincing evidence that the benefits of participating in these programs often persist over a long period of time. For example, compared to control groups, elementary school children who had been in early intervention programs were much less likely to be kept back (retained in grade) one year or more, and significantly fewer of them were placed in special classes for children with learning disabilities. They also scored higher than controls did in standard tests of reading and arithmetic achievement. At least some of the programs produced enduring increments of IQ. Palmer therefore concluded that "early intervention *can* significantly affect IQs, but it does not always."*

Apparently, early intervention programs, if well conceived and carried out, can produce marked improvements in cognitive and scholastic performance, and at least some of these are lasting. It must be reiterated, however, that these positive changes were not simply the results of attendance at nursery schools. Rather, the changes were consequences of intensive individualized work with the children, based on their needs, interests, and abilities. In some programs, participation of mothers was of paramount importance. Effective programs require meticulous planning and implementation, and they cost a great deal of time, effort, and money. Nevertheless, the outcomes of some of them are sufficiently promising, for the individual and society, to justify the expense and the effort.

* F. Palmer (unpublished report, September 1977).

Personality Development: Biological and Cultural Influences

Personality is a broad and comprehensive concept that refers to the enduring organization of the individual's predispositions, characteristics (traits), motivations, values, and ways of adjusting to the environment. Personality development is an enormously complicated process, shaped by a vast number of interrelated and continually interacting factors. At least four broad types of factors play a role in determining a child's personality characteristics and behavior. The first type is *biological* and includes genetic endowment, temperament, physical appearance, and rate of maturation. The second major category is *cultural-group membership*. Each culture has a "typical" personality—a particular pattern of motives, goals, ideals, and values—which is characteristic and distinctive of that culture and which children growing up in that culture acquire. The Japanese are generally more "group oriented," interdependent in their relations with other people, self-effacing, and passive; Americans are more independent, self-assertive, and aggressive. Obviously, children in Japanese and American cultures are brought up in different ways to achieve these cultural differences in personality. Analogously, within the American scene, many Zuñi Indian children, reared in traditional ways—often on reservations—are trained to be cooperative and egalitarian, uninterested in personal aggrandizement and achievement. In contrast, most white middle-class parents are likely to foster the development of achievement motivation in their children.

The third and, in our view, most critical influence in personality development is the history of the child's experiences with others, particularly with the members of the family. Personality is largely a product of social learning, and during the earliest years, the family—parents, brothers, and sisters—creates the learning environment for the child. Parents have the most frequent and intense interactions with their children early in life; hence they regulate and modify their children's behaviors continuously. Theirs is the key role in the child's *socialization*, the process by which the child acquires behavior patterns, motives, and values that are customary and acceptable according to the standards of his or her family and social group. Familial influences on personality development are discussed in greater detail in the next chapter.

The fourth type of influence on overt behavior and personality characteristics is the *situation*, that is, the stimuli directly impinging on the individual at any particular time. The other people present, the child's feelings of the moment (for instance, fatigue, frustration, anxiety, calm, or a happy mood), and the immediate rewards and punishments offered affect the personality characteristics and predispositions the child will manifest. Extremely active, noisy, jumpy children readily learn to be quieter and more restrained in the schoolroom if they have strict teachers. When children encounter new situations in which their habitual reactions and patterns of response are not acceptable, they will try new and different behaviors. If these new responses are rewarded, their characteristic responses may be modified substantially. This fact underlies the use of the techniques of behavior therapy, which we shall discuss later.

All these forces are interwoven—operating, interacting, and affecting personality development concurrently. Thus, although cultural-group membership and relationships with parents are central in shaping the child's personality and behavior, their effects may be tempered by the child's energy and activity levels, which are, at least partially, biologically determined.

It is only for convenience of exposition that the following discussion of personality development focuses on important biological and social forces one at a time. In actuality, it is often difficult to separate the effects of one determinant from those of another.

BIOLOGICAL FACTORS

Genetic Influences on Personality and Behavior

As we noted earlier, it is almost impossible to separate hereditary and environmental influences on human behavior, because every manifest characteristic or trait is a product of complex interactions between genetically determined potentialities and environmental forces. There is solid experimental evidence, however, that certain characteristics of dogs and other animals—such as aggressiveness, nervousness, timidity, sociability, and trainability—are strongly influenced by genetic endowment. Selective breeding can produce litters of mild, calm dogs or nervous, aggressive ones. Cocker spaniels are easy to train, relatively unemotional, and exhibit little fear, while beagles and terriers are difficult to train and more fearful.

Are comparable characteristics in humans transmitted genetically? While intelligence is to some extent under genetic control, the role of hereditary endowment in determining other aspects of psychological functioning is not so clear. Some features of personality appear to be influenced at least indirectly by these factors. For example, intensive longitudinal observations of a large group of infants, extending from the age of 2 or 3 months until 2 years, indicate that certain "intrinsic reaction types," manifested very early, are apt to persist. The variables constituting these "types" include activity or passivity, intensity of reaction, approach or withdrawal tendencies, positive or negative moods, distractability, and regularity or irregularity. It is impossible to determine whether these enduring patterns are genetically determined or learned very early, but the investigators are convinced that these are, in fact, innate and unlearned; some children more than others, they feel, are endowed with greater tendencies toward, say, activity, distractability, and strong reactions.

One of the principal means of assessing the relative contributions of heredity and environment to the development of a particular trait is to measure the extent of family resemblance or similarity in that trait. In our discussion of genetic influences on intelligence we noted that *monozygotic*, or *identical*, twins develop from a single fertilized egg and thus have exactly the same genetic constitution. *Fraternal*, or *dizygotic*, twins are the products of two eggs and thus differ genetically, although they share some genes. Therefore, if the similarities between identical twins in a trait are greater than the similarities between fraternal twins, we infer that the trait is strongly influenced by genetic factors. The assumption is made that the members of each pair of twins, identical or fraternal, share similar environments and experiences. If identical and fraternal twins resemble each other to the same degree in a characteristic, we conclude that this characteristic is more strongly influenced by environmental than by genetic factors.

Family studies of this sort show that tendencies toward inhibition and social introversion (or extroversion) may be partially under genetic control; identical twins are more similar to each other than fraternal twins in these traits. As infants, identical twins are more alike than fraternal twins in tendencies to smile and to show fear of strangers. Findings consistent with these come from studies of high school students who responded to personality questionnaires. Identical twins resembled each other much more than fraternal twins did in measures of introversion-extroversion, aggressiveness, moodiness, dependency, and shyness. These data strongly suggest that heredity contributes to the development of these characteristics.

Some mental disorders appear to have genetic components. This is true of schizophrenia, a profound psychosis characterized by severe impairments in logical thinking and in emotional relationships with others, loss of contact with reality, and marked withdrawal. One investigator examined thousands of records of schizophrenic patients to determine how many of them had twin siblings, either identical or fraternal. Then he found out whether or not the other twin was also schizophrenic. Of the identical cases, 86 percent had schizophrenic twins; only 15 percent of the twins of the fraternals were schizophrenic. Such a large difference between the two kinds of twins indicates that genetic factors contribute to the development of this emotional disorder, but the data should not be interpreted to mean that schizophrenia is directly inherited. Rather, there appears to be a genetic *predisposition* to respond with schizophrenic reactions to strong environmental stress; if the individual with such a predisposition is exposed to the appropriate environmental conditions, he or she is more likely to become schizophrenic than someone not so predisposed. Manic-depressive psychosis, characterized by mood swings from deep depression and apathy to high elation and excitement, is also influenced by genetic endowment, although the evidence is not so strong as it is in the case of schizophrenia.

Some mental illnesses of childhood *may* have a genetic basis, although the evidence is not clear-cut. For example, the *autistic child* is "different" from the very first days of life, avoiding contact with others, forming no relationships—no social smiles, no recognition of family members, no social games. The autistic child seems lonely and isolated; the child's language and speech are distorted and often unintelligible, and not ordinarily used for communication with others. Autism can be differentiated from *childhood schizophrenia*, which generally does not develop until the child is about 5 or 6 years of age. Ordinarily, the schizophrenic child speaks, while the autistic one does not. Many authorities maintain that both of these childhood mental illnesses have strong genetic components, but the genetic contributions have not been assessed precisely and the genetic mechanisms involved in the transmission of these illnesses have not been specified.

Influences of Other Biological Factors

Other biological factors also exert direct or indirect influences on personality development. For example, an overactive thyroid gland may produce hyperactivity, excitability, jumpiness, tenseness, and nervousness. People with underactive thyroid glands (too little thyroid secretion) tend to be placid, easily tired, listless, lacking in energy, and apathetic. Testosterone secretions (secretions from the male sex glands, the testes) are related to aggressivity and sexual arousal in animals, but it is not clear that this relationship holds in the case of humans.

Physical appearance, beauty or homeliness, and physique—all characteristics that are dependent on genetic constitution—may have indirect impact on personality and self-confidence. We all know of people who, because of physical attractiveness, achieve goals or positions they might not otherwise have attained, or who, because of ugliness or deformity, become profoundly unhappy, shy, or withdrawn. In the world of young boys, physical strength and prowess bring prestige and success. Those who are advanced in development, tall and muscular for their age, are more likely to be self-confident, outgoing leaders. Furthermore, these boys are likely to mature faster and have earlier growth spurts than others, so they are in a good position to maintain their predominance. Lanky boys with relatively poor muscular development are less likely to be able to hold their own in sports or rough-and-tumble play. Furthermore, these boys tend to mature more slowly, so they see others surpass them in size and athletic skill, and perhaps in social development, during early adolescence. This experience is likely to reinforce early-established negative self-concepts.

Of course, these effects may be exaggerated or mitigated by other factors. The tall, well-built, strong boy is not likely to become secure and self-confident if he happens to be unintelligent and unsuccessful in school or if, as a result of his relationships at home, he is insecure and dependent. On the other hand, if the weak, unattractive boy is bright and academically successful or has stable, reassuring relationships at home, he may not become insecure in spite of the fact that his physical appearance initially arouses unfavorable reactions from his peers.

Systematic studies of normal children show that there are small but significant relationships between body build and personality. Among 10- and 11-year-olds, small, poorly coordinated, and relatively weak children are inclined to be timid, fearful, passive, and generally worried. In contrast, tall, strong, energetic, well-coordinated children of the same age are playful, self-expressive, talkative, productive, and creative.

It hardly seems likely that the genetic or constitutional factors that help determine physical characteristics also have direct impacts on personality traits. Rather, some features of physique may affect the individual's capabilities, aptitudes, and interests; most critically, peers' and adults' reactions to the child are affected by his or her appearance. To illustrate, in our culture peers and adults are likely to react to a small, awkward, physically weak boy as though he were delicate, sensitive, dependent, unaggressive, and perhaps lacking in competence. Furthermore, since this boy is not likely to be success-ful in physical games and athletics, he is not likely to develop intense interests in these activities and may begin to withdraw from others, as well as from physical activities. Not surprisingly, he may become timid, passive, and dependent.

Tall, strong, well-coordinated boys, on the other hand, are likely to be considered more mature, independent, aggressive, and competent. In addition, these children are likely to be skillful in motor activities, successful in athletics, and energetic in social inter-actions. For these reasons they may be accorded high social status and may therefore develop self-confidence and outgoing character-istics. In sum, a child's physical characteristics may affect his or her approach to the social environment, the expectancies of others, and their reactions. These, in turn, may have impacts on the child's personality development.

Rate of Maturation

Some adolescents reach physical maturity relatively early; oth-ers are quite delayed. These individual differences are attributable, in large part, to gentically determined hormonal functions. From the point of view of personality development, it is significant that the social-psychological environments encountered by adolescents may vary considerably, depending on their rate of physical maturation. A late-maturing boy looks young for his age and is likely to be re-garded and treated as immature by others. He may sometimes doubt whether his body will ever develop properly and whether he will be as well endowed sexually as others he sees developing around him. The early-maturing boy, on the other hand, clearly sees his own growth and his own physical changes leading to adulthood. Others regard him as more grown up socially and emotionally, and he has an advantage over the late-maturing boy in competitive athletics, which continue to be important at this age.

The psychological consequences of these differences have been demonstrated in studies comparing the personalities of late- and early-maturing adolescent boys. Those who are relatively retarded physically tend to reveal more maladjustment. They have some negative self-concepts, harbor stronger feelings of inadequacy and rejection, and are both more dependent and more rebellious. In contrast, the early maturing boys generally feel adequate, accepted by others, self-confident, independent, mature, and capable of playing an adult role; apparently, these boys are more likely than the others to live in circumstances that are conducive to good psychological adjustment.

Among girls, early maturing—at the age of 11 or 12—may be a slight handicap socially. Some girls are embarrassed by their early maturation. But beginning with the seventh grade and throughout the junior high school years, early maturing becomes a social advantage and is associated with being popular and highly regarded by peers. The findings about the effects of early and late maturing must be interpreted cautiously, however, for

> although rate of maturing and associated factors may affect personality development, the relationship between physical status and psychological characteristics is by no means simple. A vast number of complex, interacting factors, including rate of maturation, determine each adolescent's unique personality structure. Hence, in any specific instance, the group findings . . . may not be directly applicable, for other physical, psychological, or social factors may attenuate the effects of late- or early-maturing. For example, an adolescent boy who is fundamentally secure and has warm, accepting parents and generally rewarding social relationships may not develop strong feelings of inadequacy even if he matures slowly. Analogously, the early-maturing boy who has deep feelings of insecurity, for whatever reasons, will probably not gain self-confidence simply because he matures early. In summary, in understanding any individual case, generalizations based on [these] data . . . must be particularized in the light of the individual's past history and present circumstances.*

SOCIALIZATION AND CULTURAL INFLUENCES ON PERSONALITY

From the point of view of personality development, the most significant aspect of a child's world is his or her *social* environment. Virtually all human beings live in a society, an interacting group of people. And each society has a distinctive culture, a body of stored

* P. H. Mussen and M. C. Jones, "Self-Conceptions, Motivations, and Interpersonal Attitudes of Late- and Early-Maturing Boys," *Child Development*, 28 (June 1957), 255.

knowledge, characteristic ways of thinking and feeling, attitudes, goals, and ideals.

"Culture regulates our lives at every turn. From the moment we are born until we die there is, whether we are conscious of it or not, constant pressure upon us to follow certain types of behavior that other men have created for us."* How does an individual's cultural-group membership influence the development of his or her personality? Primarily by prescribing—and limiting—what children are taught and what they learn. As we shall demonstrate, each culture expects, and trains, its members to behave in the ways that are acceptable to the group. To a marked degree, children's cultural groups define the range of experiences and situations they are likely to encounter and the values and personality characteristics that are reinforced and hence learned. Each culture has its own concepts and specific techniques of child rearing, as well as a set of expectations regarding patterns of approved behavior.

Socialization

Socialization is the process by which individuals acquire, from the enormously wide range of behavioral potentialities that are open to them at birth, those behavior patterns that are customary and acceptable according to the standards of their families and social groups. Within the limits set by their hereditary endowments and abilities, children in a complex and varied culture can become almost any type of person: aggressive or mild, competitive or cooperative, meat-eating or vegetarian, motivated toward or uninterested in intellectual achievement, sexually expressive or inhibited, dependent or independent, honest or dishonest, politically liberal or reactionary. The possibilities are, in effect, almost infinite; yet ordinarily any individual adopts only the behavior deemed appropriate for his or her own social, ethnic, and religious groups. How this occurs is the core problem in studying the process of socialization.

The culture in which the child grows up prescribes, to a considerable degree, the *methods* and *goals* of socialization—that is, *how* he or she is trained and *which* personality characteristics, motives, attitudes, and values are adopted. There are, of course, universal aspects of socialization; every culture makes provisions for maintaining and perpetuating itself, for establishing an orderly way of life, and for satisfying the biological needs of its members. In all cultures, children must be fed, toilet trained, and protected from

* C. Kluckhohn, *Mirror for Man* (New York: McGraw-Hill, 1949), p. 327.

illness. No culture can survive and endure unless aggressive and sexual impulses and dependency are to some extent controlled, although cultures differ widely in their permissiveness (or restrictiveness) of expression of these motives.

There are numberless variations in the methods cultures use for achieving these and other important goals. The standard or prescribed ways of taking care of children vary greatly from culture to culture. In most cultures the child has one primary caretaker, usually the mother (monomatric societies), but there are cultures in which many women participate in a child's upbringing (polymatric cultures). In some cultures, infants are always handled gently and their needs are met promptly and completely, whereas in other cultures the infant is frequently and severely frustrated. Most American babies are breast-fed for only a few months; but in some African cultures children are permitted to nurse until they are 5 or 6 years old. The culture may prescribe that toilet training be accomplished gradually, or babies may be expected to achieve bladder and bowel control by the age of 6 months and punished if they have accidents after that. Of course, every culture's ways of handling child rearing have a specific goal: facilitating the acquisition of culturally approved patterns of personality characteristics, motivation, attitudes, and values—in other words, producing individuals with personality structures that fit into the culture and help maintain it.

Training to accomplish these goals begins very early. For example, within the first three months Japanese infants start their training to become group-oriented, interdependent in their relationships with others, and passive, while American babies begin to learn independence and self-assertion. American mothers are more lively and stimulating in their approaches to their babies, moving them about, looking at them, and vocalizing more in attempts to excite their interests. Japanese mothers, in contrast, spend more time with their babies in general, talk with them to soothe them when they are fussy, and have a generally quieting approach toward their babies. By the age of 3 or 4 months, the infants already respond in culturally appropriate ways.

> The Japanese boy baby seems passive, and he lies quietly with occasional unhappy vocalizations, while his mother, in her care, does more lulling, carrying, and rocking of her baby. She seems to try to soothe and quiet the child and to communicate with him physically rather than verbally. On the other hand, the American infant is more active, happily vocal, and exploring of his environment, and his mother in her care does more looking at and chatting to her baby. She seems to stimulate the baby to activity and to vocal response. It is as if the American mother

wanted to have a vocal, active baby, and the Japanese mother wanted to have a quiet, contented baby. In terms of the styles of caretaking of the mothers in the two cultures, they seem to get what they apparently want.*

Later training for the culturally approved patterns of behavior and social interrelationships is generally consistent with the earliest training given by parents, even though it may be given by others—by older brothers and sisters, relatives, teachers, or religious leaders. Thus, in Japan the child's later experiences lead toward increasing interdependence in social relationships, while the American path very early leads toward increasing independence from others. Thus, in the American family the child is likely to be separated from the family in sleeping arrangements within the first few years of life, while the Japanese child continues to sleep with his or her parents during the transition from infancy to childhood and is very likely to sleep with a brother or sister until approximately the age of 15.

Throughout their childhood, American children are encouraged to be self-reliant and independent and at the same time to deny feelings of dependency. Asking for help may provoke anxiety or feelings of inadequacy in American children and adolescents. In traditional Chinese culture, on the other hand, independence is not so highly prized, and asking for help is not so likely to produce feelings of inferiority.

General American culture—middle-class American culture in particular—stresses competition and personal achievement. Early in life, American children are made aware of the value of accomplishment, and as they grow older rewards for competition increase and competitive attitudes become stronger. In contrast, sharing and cooperation are stressed by the Hopi Indians and on Israeli kibbutzim (collective farms), and from an early age children in these cultures are discouraged from competing. In American schoolrooms, competition has traditionally been a powerful motive for doing good work rapidly and efficiently; among the Hopi, children who complete their work quickly are likely to "hold back," for they are reluctant to embarrass others. White Americans are likely to strive to achieve "leading" positions in school or community, but Hopi children refuse such honors, preferring to remain equal, but not superior, to their peers.

* W. Caudill and H. Weinstein, "Maternal Care and Infant Behavior in Japan and America," in *Readings in Child Behavior and Development*, 3rd ed., ed. C. S. Lavatelli and F. Stendler (New York: Harcourt Brace Jovanovich, 1972), p. 84.

Sex Typing

In all cultures, certain work tasks and activities are assigned to men, others to women. But the nature of the assignment varies from culture to culture. Cooking, care of domestic animals, and weaving are women's activities in some cultures, but they are men's duties in others. Aggression, self-reliance, and independence are defined as masculine attributes in most cultures, while nurturance, obedience, and responsibility are considered feminine traits. There are many exceptions, however. Among the Tchambuli, a New Guinea tribe studied by the renowned anthropologist Margaret Mead, females are trained to be aggressive and dominating while the males learn to be emotionally dependent, nurturant, and sensitive. Members of two other tribes that live on the same island, just a few miles away, have vastly different ideas about sex-appropriate behavior. Among the Arapesh, individuals of both sexes are passive and gentle; both men and women of the Mundugamor tribe are hostile and suspicious.

Consider also the radical changes in the definitions of sex-appropriate behavior in American culture in recent years. Traditional sex-role differentiations, particularly in the areas of work and education, have broken down to a great extent, and personality characteristics are less rigidly defined as masculine or feminine. Such cultural and historical variations in the definitions of sex-appropriate behavior and traits testify that it is the culture, not biological sex, that determines the roles and characteristics assigned to men and women. There is no biological basis for many of the standard or stereotyped patterns of "masculine" and "feminine" characteristics; it is not destined by nature that females be passive, dependent, and noncompetitive or that they play down their intellectual potential and devote themselves exclusively to home and family.

Adolescence in Different Cultures

In some societies, such as American, the transition from childhood to adulthood is relatively abrupt and difficult. During adolescence, many new tasks must be learned rapidly and new responses must be acquired within a short period of time. American culture demands that the adolescent resolve many problems simultaneously—achieving some independence from family; choosing and preparing for a vocation; and making a mature, heterosexual adjustment, including the setting up of a separate household. The culture insists that adolescents cope with all these problems, even though

63

they may wish to remain secure, dependent, and free of responsibility. Under the circumstances, it is not surprising that in American culture adolescence is often a period of stress, conflict, and emotional upset. In fact, in what seems to be the classical—or, at least, Western—view, adolescence is a time of "storm and stress," of contradictory needs and desires, of emotional instability, and of rebellion from parents and authority. Many psychologists concluded that emotional disturbance was a universal and inevitable characteristic of this period of development.

Preparation for adulthood—for independence, for vocation, for sexual maturity—is much more gradual and less complicated in some other societies, and in these societies there is much less turmoil during adolescence. Margaret Mead pointed this out many years ago when she conducted research in Samoa, where adolescence is a relatively relaxed and happy time. The general course of development in Samoa is gradual, smooth, and uncomplicated; there are no abrupt leaps into the adult world and into new roles and responsibilities. Samoan children learn about sex very early in life. By adolescence, boys and girls are sexually active, experimenting and exploring sexual relationships without hesitancy or guilt. As Mead put it, "adolescence represented no period of crisis or stress but instead an orderly developing of a set of slowly maturing interests and activities."*

In other societies the child prepares much more gradually for independence, for his or her vocational role, and for mature sexuality. Among the Indians of Mexico, for example, young children are treated with great leniency and have few assigned duties, but they soon begin to take on some of the necessary work of the community. By the age of 6 or 7, the typical Mexican Indian girl begins to care for her younger brothers and sisters, goes to the market, and helps to serve food and wash dishes. Boys of the same age begin to help gather food in the fields and to care for large animals such as goats and donkeys. Gradually they take increasing responsibility and perform the work they will assume as adults. Parents are nurturant and do not pressure their children to do jobs beyond their capabilities, but they expect them to do some essential work they are capable of doing. In Mexican Indian culture, adolescence is not likely to be a period of stress or conflict. Adolescents in Israeli kibbutzim, living communally in youth societies, show relatively little emotional disturbance or rebellion from their elders and enter smoothly into adult society.

* M. Mead, *Coming of Age in Samoa* (New York: William Morrow & Co., 1928), p. 157.

Adjustment to mature sexuality is also conditioned by cultural factors. Traditionally, American middle-class sex training has been highly restrictive; children and adolescents are supposed to inhibit sexual responses, including even thoughts about sex. Yet adults are supposed to reverse these early-established attitudes suddenly and to enjoy sexual activity after they are married. As a result, conflicts about sex are common; early learning of sexual inhibition and anxiety about sex may be very difficult to overcome.

In contrast, the children of one African society are expected to begin preparing for mature sexual functioning from an early age. In this society, 9- and 10-year-old children build little huts outside the village, and with complete approval of their parents, boys and girls begin to play at being husband and wife. These boy-girl sexual relationships may extend into adolescence, although there are often exchanges of partners until marriage. In societies such as these there are few problems of adult sexual adjustment.

Social-Class Differences

American culture is not an undifferentiated entity; it is a complex, differentiated, pluralistic society, stratified along ethnic and socioeconomic lines—with many social inequalities related to this stratification—and undergoing rapid change. Each ethnic and socioeconomic group has its own distinct culture, philosophy of life, system of values, and patterns of behavior. Children in different segments of American society have different child-rearing experiences, different opportunities, and different rewards, and consequently they differ in personality structure, behavior, and attitudes.

By the time they enter school, children are keenly aware of class distinctions and of their own relative positions in the social hierarchy. Middle-class people in American society can satisfy most of their basic needs without great difficulty, and they are apt to share the values of the society. Poor people, however, must worry about the basic necessities, food and shelter, and they feel fundamentally powerless, ineffective in influencing or shaping their destinies or the society of which they are part. These attitudes are communicated to their children, and as might be expected, black children and lower-class white children score lower on tests of self-esteem and self-assurance than white middle-class children. Furthermore, lower-class children, particularly blacks, have much less sense of personal efficacy; they are much less inclined than middle-class children to believe that their own actions determine what happens to them and, rather, see their lives as controlled by external events.

Compared with lower-class parents, those of the middle class have high expectations for their children and make greater demands, stressing independence, self-reliance, the achievement of high goals, educational accomplishments, and the ability to delay gratification (that is, to sacrifice immediate goals to obtain more substantial long-term objectives). Both observational and experimental studies indicate that lower-class children develop relatively little capacity to delay gratification, because for them the future is uncertain and they are frequently frustrated in attempting to satisfy their basic needs. Since they cannot depend on future gratifications, they act in accordance with the philosophy that "a bird in the hand is worth two in the bush."

Physical aggression seems to play a larger part in the lives of lower-class people than in those of middle-class people; lower-class children have generally been found to be more physically aggressive and belligerent than middle-class children. Sexual expression is also less inhibited in the lower class, and many more lower-class than middle-class adolescents have sexual intercourse.

Lower-class adults tend to think of personal relationships in terms of power. They have very little voice in decisions that affect their daily lives, and in their work they are usually directed and supervised by others. Advancement in rank or wages is more likely to be due to group efforts (for example, unions) than to individual initiative. In contrast, the work of the middle-class adult is more likely to involve some policy making, self-direction, and autonomy; success in work is more likely to be the result of one's own initiative and skill. These social-class differences in life style and philosophy are reflected in techniques of child rearing and training. The power orientation of lower-class parents is manifested in their frequent use of direct demands, threats, deprivation, and coercive punishment in disciplining young children, although these parents are apt to become more permissive when their children are older. Middle-class parents, being more concerned with personal feelings and social relationships, are more likely to be permissive with infants and young children, using love-oriented discipline (withdrawal of affection, disapproval, shame, guilt) to influence behavior; but they exert greater controls and give more supervision when their children are adolescents.

As would be expected, middle-class parents stress achievement motivation, learning, and educational accomplishment much more than lower-class parents. In one study, black mothers from four different social classes were asked to teach their 4-year-old children several tasks that they themselves had been taught by the investigator.

Middle-class mothers were more likely to provide an orientation to the task for the child, to request verbal feedback rather than physical compliance, to be specific in their instructions, to use motivation techniques that involved explicit or implicit reward, and, on a number of measures, to provide the child with information he needed to complete the task and to monitor his performance.

These studies of observed maternal behavior agree in their portrayal of middle-class mothers as more attentive and more responsive to their children, and apparently more aware of their children's feelings and perspectives on the activities in which they are engaged. . . . They also tend less to use power-oriented punishment in influence techniques, are more likely to explain to the child the rationale involved in a request and to provide ideas and words through which maternal control can be mediated.*

Ethnic groups within a society also differ markedly in their emphasis on achievement motivation. For example, a large number of mothers and sons from six American ethnic groups—French Canadians, southern Italians, Greeks, Eastern European Jews, northeastern U.S. blacks, and native-born white Protestants—were interviewed about independence training, orientations toward achievement, and vocational and occupational aspirations. Jewish mothers expressed the highest aspirations for their sons and expected them to be independent and self-reliant at a relatively early age. These mothers, as well as Greek, white Protestant, and black mothers, encouraged active, future-oriented, individualistic values and had higher educational and occupational aspirations for their sons than did southern Italian and French-Canadian mothers. Although black mothers also expressed individualistic goals and high educational aspirations for their sons, they had, probably realistically, the lowest occupational goals of all the groups. As would be predicted from their mothers' attitudes and aspirations, the Jewish, Greek, and white Protestant boys had higher achievement motivation than did Italians, French Canadians, and blacks.

* R. D. Hess, "Class and Ethnic Influences upon Socialization," in *Carmichael's Manual of Child Psychology*, 3rd ed., ed. P. Mussen (New York: John Wiley & Sons, 1970), p. 480.

Personality Development: Familial, Peer, and Situational Influences

As our discussion has made clear, socialization is strongly influenced by *cultural prescriptions*. These prescriptions must, however, be initially communicated by members of the child's family, the representatives of the culture with whom he or she has the most intimate relationships.

THE FAMILY

Children's first social learning occurs at home; their earliest experiences with their families—particularly the bonds with their mothers—are generally assumed to be critical antecedents of later social relationships.

Typically, the mother gratifies her infant's primary needs for food, for alleviation of pain, for warmth, and perhaps even for tactile stimulation (which may be a basic, innate drive). Consequently, the mother's presence—the visual, auditory, tactile, and kinesthetic stimuli she presents—becomes associated with the satisfaction of needs, and she begins to stand for pleasure, relief of tension, and contentment.

The earliest meaningful mother-child relationship has generally been referred to as *attachment*, or sometimes *dependency*, which is actually a reciprocal relationship. "The helpless infant elicits care-taking and other responses from the mother and the mother in turn evokes visual regard, vocalization, smiles and approach movements from the infant. These infant responses in turn stimulate further nurturant and affectionate behavior in the mother."*

During the first few months of life, infants are indiscriminate in social responsiveness, smiling in response to everyone and every smiling face. Beginning about the age of 6 or 7 months, however, they begin to differentiate between their mothers and other people. They react especially favorably toward their mothers, smiling and vocalizing more toward them than toward others, showing greater preference for them and more initiative in making contact with them, and looking at them for longer periods of time and being readily soothed by them. As the infant forms a more elaborate and coherent concept of the mother, he or she begins to develop certain expectations of her, seeking to be near her and approaching her when under any condition of stress—hungry, in pain, uncomfortable, or afraid. If the mother is nurturant and attends to her child's needs promptly and effectively, she rewards these approach responses, and these are likely to be repeated. When children 9 or 10 months of age are put into a room with attractive toys but without their mothers or caretakers, most of them show considerable distress, often crying and refusing to explore the room. On the other hand, if their caretakers remain in the room with them, children this age explore freely and vocalize pleasantly; under these conditions, they are also less wary of strangers. In a new environment, children between 18 and 30 months spend more time in play if they can readily see their mothers and make visual contact with them (if they are seated on the other side of the room rather than behind the child or behind a screen). They do not actually look at her more; rather, knowing that she is there enables them to play freely. Infants apparently derive security from the presence of their caretakers and the opportunity to be in contact with them.

Attachment refers to an enduring relationship between a caretaker (usually the mother) and the child, in which the caretaker is preferred to others, contact with her is sought, and she serves as a secure base for exploration. There are marked individual differences in the *quality* of mother-infant attachments. Some babies are strongly and securely attached to their mothers; some have only weak attachments. Securely attached infants regard the mother as a secure base; when she is present, they explore the environment without anxiety, looking back at her and returning to her from time to time.

Differences in the *quality* of the infants' attachment cannot be

* L. J. Yarrow and F. A. Pedersen, "Attachment: Its Origins and Course," in *The Young Child: Reviews of Research*, ed. W. W. Hartup (Washington, D.C.: National Association for the Education of Young Children, 1972), p. 54.

assessed directly but can be inferred from observations of caretaker-infant interactions. In the most systematic studies of this issue, Mary Ainsworth and her colleagues made use of a standard, controlled "strange situation." The mother and her 1-year-old baby were first brought into the unfamiliar room in which there was an array of attractive toys. After a short period (three minutes), a stranger entered the room and approached the baby; then the mother left, leaving the baby with the stranger; when the mother returned, the stranger departed. Particular attention was paid to the child's reactions at the time of the mother's return. *Securely attached* children exhibited more attachment behavior when they were reunited with their mothers; that is, the infants made more vigorous attempts to be near her and to remain in contact with her. Less securely attached babies showed different reactions. Some of them were *avoidant*, keeping away or ignoring her; others seemed to be in conflict, approaching her and seeking contact at first, and then trying to get away from her by turning, crawling, or looking away. Another group of babies showed both attachment behavior *and* anger; their interactions were clearly *ambivalent*.

What determines the quality of the mother-child attachment? According to Ainsworth, the critical variable is the mother's reactions to her child's needs. Mothers of the securely attached infants were generally sensitive, cooperative, accepting, and accessible in their interactions with their babies. The mothers of avoidant babies, in contrast, were rejecting, insensitive, unresponsive women who were often inaccessible when their children needed them and frequently interfered with their babies' activities. A baby becomes securely attached to a mother who "is accessible enough to receive the baby's signals, ... can interpret them accurately and ... her response to them is prompt and appropriate."[*]

The quality of the child's attachment appears to be stable at least throughout infancy. Of 50 infants classified into the categories "securely attached," "avoidant," or "ambivalent" at 12 months of age, 48 were again classified the same way, totally independently, at 18 months of age.

The quality of early attachment is correlated with some of the child's subsequent cognitive and emotional characteristics. Babies who were securely attached at 12 months of age scored higher than others on intelligence tests and were more compliant with their mothers' requests at age 2. When compared with securely attached babies, infants classified as avoidant at 12 or 18 months were more

[*] M. D. S. Ainsworth, "The Development of Infant-Mother Attachment," in *Review of Child Development Research*, Vol. 3, ed. B. M. Caldwell and H. N. Ricciuti (Chicago: University of Chicago Press, 1973), p. 49.

likely to be negativistic or noncompliant (doing the opposite of what they were requested to do), or only partially compliant, with requests. In an experimental setting, they were more likely to seek help from an experimenter than from their mothers.

According to many theorists and clinicians, the development of attachment—and the interdependence and intense feeling involved—

is the foundation of a *sense of trust* in others and in the world. If the mother is the source of rewarding, gratifying experiences, the infant will trust her. This trust will generalize to others and will be reflected in favorable social attitudes and friendly, outgoing approaches to other people. In contrast, a mother who is not dependable, and does not minister to the infant's needs promptly or adequately, does not evoke attachment from her child. Rather, her neglect produces distrust in the child, which is then generalized to others.

Erik Erikson, the well-known psychoanalyst, states that

> experiences connected with feeding are a prime source for the development of trust. At around four months of age a hungry baby will grow quiet and show signs of pleasure at the sound of an approaching footstep, anticipating (trusting) that he will be held and fed. This repeated experience of being hungry, seeing food, receiving food, and feeling relieved and comforted assures the baby that the world is a dependable place.*

Other developmental psychologists agree with Erikson's ideas:

> The development of specific expectations towards the mother is followed by the emergence of a higher level of relationship, the development of confidence or trust. The infant shows this trust by being able to wait if expected gratifications are not immediately forthcoming. He has the confident expectation that his mother will respond to him in predictable ways, that she will soothe him, or provide the objects necessary for his gratification. This trust is associated with strong affective involvement and mutual interdependence. At a later age, he evidences confidence in leaving the mother and exploring a strange environment, secure in the knowledge that his mother will be there to comfort him. Although the quality of attachment changes throughout the developmental cycle, trust and positive emotional involvement remain the core elements.†

These writings clearly imply that strong attachments to the mother during infancy have positive effects on the infant's subsequent development and adjustment. Indeed, there is substantial evidence that supports this view. Infants reared in emotionally cold and unstimulating environments—for example, in institutions where the

---

* E. Erikson, "The Course of Healthy Personality Development" (Midcentury White House Conference on Children and Youth), in *The Adolescent: A Book of Readings,* ed. J. M. Seidman (New York: Holt, Rinehart & Winston, 1960), p. 219.

† Yarrow and Pedersen, "Attachment," p. 59.

care is routine and there is very little individual attention—do not readily form attachments to others. Pediatricians have noted that infants reared in such settings tend to be quiet, passive, inactive, unhappy, and emotionally disturbed.

Systematic studies reinforce these clinical findings, showing that early attachment to the mother—or to a mother substitute (surrogate)—generally benefits the infant, while failure to develop such attachments has immediate and enduring adverse consequences. In one study, infant orphans who had been reared in a deprived, psychologically inadequate institution during the first few months of their lives were moved to a more stimulating setting. Each child was cared for by one caretaker, talked to, played with, and given toys. These children improved markedly in mental alertness and in intelligence; in a year, the average gain in intelligence-test score was 27 points. A control group of children, who remained in the unstimulating institution, showed an average decline of 16 points during the same period.

Other consequences of emotionally inadequate rearing of infants were demonstrated in a study conducted in Iran. Infants in a deprived orphanage who were handled impersonally, had no toys, and had little opportunity to practice motor activities were compared with a group in a more stimulating orphanage who received more personal attention, had more toys, and enjoyed greater opportunities for motor practice. The children in the stimulating orphanage were considerably more content, emotionally more mature, and happier than the others, and during their second year they were more advanced in motor ability.

It is possible to do interesting experimental work and to be very humane at the same time, as the following study shows. A kindly woman psychologist became the "mother" of eight babies in an orphanage for eight weeks. She established a warm, intimate relationship with each of her charges, attended to their needs personally for eight hours a day, played with them, smiled, cooed, and talked to them. A control group of eight infants was handled in a routine, impersonal, though kindly, way by various members of the staff of the institution. These latter infants had little individualized attention and formed no attachments to adults. The two groups of infants showed pronounced behavioral differences by the end of the experimental period. Those who had become attached to their mother surrogate were friendly and outgoing, vocalizing, cooing, and smiling when the experimenter-mother or strangers smiled at them or talked to them. The controls were much less sociable and gave much less evidence of being interested in others.

Long-Term Effects
of Early Maternal Treatment

Failure to develop strong attachment to the mother early in infancy may also have very important adverse long-term effects. Harry Harlow of the University of Wisconsin, an eminent researcher in primate behavior, kept some monkey infants of both sexes in individual wire cages so that they had no contacts with mothers during the early months of their lives; obviously, they were deprived of maternal attachment and affection. As adults, each of these socially deprived monkeys was paired with a normal monkey of the opposite sex. The deprived animals were unable to establish affectional relations or engage in normal sexual activity. For example, deprived males displayed too much aggression, made threatening gestures, and even physically attacked their female partners. Deprived females would permit normal males to come close for very brief periods of time—responding to the male initiative—but avoided being near the males for more than a minute at a time. "Evidently the failure to experience affection early in life rules out the possibility of later reproductive heterosexual relations."*

Without direct evidence, we cannot generalize from these conclusions about the effects of early affectional deprivation on sexual behavior. There is abundant evidence, however, that early institutionalization and the consequent failure to form attachments may lead to subsequent cognitive deficiencies and personality maladjustments. One investigator compared two groups of orphans reared in different settings during their first three years. The children in one group had been adopted into foster homes as young infants and had had an opportunity to form attachments to their foster mothers because they had been given individual attention, nurturance, warmth, and adequate mothering. The other group had remained in an institution for three years, receiving impersonal care and inadequate mothering; they had had no intense affectional relationships with any particular mother figure. Many of these latter children were placed in foster homes after three years in the institution.

The researcher studied the children longitudinally at four ages—3½, 6½, 8½, and 12. He observed and interviewed them, and gave them tests of intelligence, educational achievement, personality, motor coordination, social maturity, and language ability.

The institution-reared group were relatively retarded intellectually. At all ages they performed more poorly than the foster-home

* H. F. Harlow, *Learning to Love* (San Francisco: Albion Publishing Company, 1971), p. 59.

children on intelligence tests, especially in the areas of concept formation, reasoning, and abstract thinking. Language and speech difficulties were more common among the institution-reared children and persisted long after they left the orphanage.

Personality and adjustment also appeared to be affected adversely by institutional upbringing. Those reared in the orphanage were more maladjusted than the others; they lacked self-control and behaved more aggressively. They were more distractable and hyperactive, and they more frequently lied, stole, destroyed property, threw temper tantrums, and hit and kicked others. In addition, they were more dependent on adults, demanding attention frequently and asking for help unnecessarily.

Institution-reared children had not developed a basic sense of trust in others. Their social relationships were superficial, and they remained emotionally withdrawn and unresponsive, avoiding strong affectionate attachments. The investigator concluded that social and emotional maladjustment persisting into adolescence were the results of the severe deprivations and the emotional unresponsiveness of their early environment.

In interpreting these findings, we must keep in mind that these striking effects were noted among children who were *markedly* deprived of personal, warm, maternal care in the earliest years. The consequences of lesser degrees of deprivation—that is, mildly inadequate mothering, and consequently weaker attachments—are unknown.

Child-Rearing Techniques
during the Second Year

During the child's second year many new and important cognitive, motor, and language skills emerge. Children's understanding of the world increases, and their ability to think and solve problems improves. Concomitantly, they learn to walk and their manual skills and motor coordination progress rapidly; their language competence increases enormously. Two-year-olds enjoy trying out their new skills and abilities, investigating their surroundings, and testing their new capacities. If their parents encourage the children to explore freely, rewarding their curiosity and independent behavior, they are apt to continue to investigate their surroundings and attempt to manipulate the environment actively. Such children are likely to develop spontaneity, curiosity, and self-confidence, together with strong drives for autonomy, independence, mastery, competence, and achievement.

Parents who severely restrict their children's freedom of movement may inhibit their tendencies to explore and to investigate, and thus stifle the development of motivations for autonomy and independence. Some mothers find it difficult to deal with active, running, jumping, climbing children who seem to be into everything; hence, they discourage exploration and attempts to experiment. Other mothers are overprotective, tending to baby their children, discouraging independence and attempting to keep them close and clinging—perhaps because they regard independence as a threat to their own domination, control, and possession of the children. Many overprotected children become submissive and compliant; unable or afraid to make spontaneous responses; inhibited in investigating, exploring, and experimenting; and shy and withdrawn in social situations. These children lack persistence; they give up readily when faced with difficult tasks or problems, probably as a result of lack of rewards for early problem-solving efforts and because of their parents' tendency to solve problems for them. Since persistence is often necessary for learning academic subjects, an overprotected child may be at a disadvantage when he or she enters school.

Parental stimulation and encouragement of children's independent achievements, exploration, and attempts at mastery may affect their later behavior in positive ways. For example, among nursery school children, those with mothers who encourage early independence and achievement tend to be more interested than others in mastery and achievement. They spend more time in challenging and creative activities such as painting, making clay models, and reading books. When they reach school age they are, according to personality tests, more highly motivated for achievement, and their grades are better than those of children who were not rewarded for early strivings for independence. Apparently, strong motivation to learn and to perform well in school is fostered by parental encouragement of competence and exploration early in life. Moreover, motivation for achievement appears to be a stable aspect of personality. If it develops early, it is likely to be maintained over a long span of years.

The Effects of Different Types of Home Atmospheres

As children mature and grow in capability, their relationships with their parents become more complex and subtle. Broad features of the home—such as warmth, democracy, intellectuality, affectionateness, friction, permissiveness (or restrictiveness), punitiveness, firmness of discipline—begin to have profound impacts on many aspects of the child's behavior and development.

This was clearly demonstrated in a series of studies conducted by Diana Baumrind of the Institute of Human Development at the University of California at Berkeley. Baumrind focused her attention on the kinds of parent-child relationships related to competence, self-reliance, and independence in young children. Nursery school children were intensively observed and rated on scales of self-control, curiosity about new and exciting stimuli, self-reliance, and general mood (pleasure and enthusiasm). Three contrasting groups of children were delineated: first, the most self-reliant, self-controlled, explorative, and contented children; second, the discontented, withdrawn, and distrustful children; and third, the least self-reliant, explorative, and self-controlled. Visits to the children's homes and structured observations of interactions between parents and children provided the major data used to evaluate several significant aspects of child rearing—specifically, parental *control*, *maturity demands* (pressures on children to perform at the level of their ability and to make decisions on their own), *clarity of communication*, and *parental nurturance* (warmth toward, and involvement with, the child).

The results showed that the three groups of children experienced vastly different patterns of child rearing. For example, parents of children in the first group (the most mature, competent, and self-reliant) were rated high in all four parent-child dimensions; that is, these parents were controlling and demanding, but at the same time they were warm, rational, communicative, and receptive to their children's communications. The investigator labeled this pattern *authoritative*; it involves a balance between nurturance and control, high demands and clear communications, together with encouragement of the child's independent exploration.

The parents of the discontented, withdrawn, and distrustful children in the second group were themselves detached and highly controlling, less warm and more punitive than the parents in the other groups. They were called *authoritarian* parents.

Parents of children in the third group, the least self-reliant and self-controlled, were *permissive* (warm, supportive, and nurturant, but inclined to be overprotective and lax in discipline); they made few demands on their children and did little to encourage independence.

In a further study of these relationships, the investigator refined and elaborated the definitions of the three types of child rearing. She then related these practices to competence, independence, and responsibility in another large group of young boys and girls. Note the contrasts in the following summaries of the parental patterns.

Authoritarian parents attempt to shape and control the child's behavior and attitudes according to a set standard of conduct. Important virtues are obedience, respect for authority, and respect for work and for order. Punitive, forceful means are used to discipline the child; verbal give-and-take is not encouraged.

Authoritative parents, by contrast, attempt to direct the child's activity in a rational way, encouraging verbal communication and informing the child of the reasoning behind their policies. They value their child's self-expression, independence, individual interests, and unique characteristics. Hence, although they exert firm control at times, they do not hem in the child with restrictions.

Permissive parents are nonpunitive, accepting the child's impulses, desires, and actions. They make few demands on the child for responsibility or for order, allowing the child to regulate his or her own activities as much as possible. They avoid controlling the child, consult with him or her about policy decisions, and give explanations for family rules.*

The study showed clearly that *authoritative* parents were the most effective in promoting the development of competence, responsibility, and independence. High demands for maturity and firmness in disciplinary matters appear to be associated with both self-assertion and social responsibility in young children. Compared with permissive and authoritarian parents, those who are authoritative are more likely to produce responsible, friendly, cooperative, and achievement-oriented children, especially if the children are boys. The investigator suggests that although both authoritative and authoritarian parents preach responsible behavior, the latter do not practice it; they are more concerned with their own ideas and standards than with the child's interests and welfare. Authoritative parents, on the other hand, both preach and practice responsible behavior; hence, their children behave more responsibly. Permissive parents do little to encourage or reward responsible behavior or to discourage immature behavior. Their children are clearly lacking in responsibility and achievement-oriented behavior.

Independence and achievement orientation in girls are clearly associated with authoritative upbringing; in boys, nonconforming parental behavior and, to a lesser extent, authoritative upbringing are associated with these characteristics. The investigator concluded that

> parents who provided the most enriched environment, namely the nonconforming and the authoritative parents, had the most dominant and purposive children. These parents, by comparison with the others

* Descriptions of parents summarized from D. Baumrind, "Authoritarian vs. Authoritative Parent Control," *Adolescence*, 3 (1968), 255–72.

studied, set high standards of excellence, invoked cognitive insight, provided an intellectually stimulating atmosphere, were themselves rated as being differentiated and individualistic, and made high educational demands upon the child.*

Warmth, support, and nurturance from the parents are critical antecedents of children's maturity, independence, self-reliance, competence, and responsibility. But love and support are not enough to assure the development of these characteristics. Other prerequisites are adequate communication between parents and children; the use of reason rather than punishment in achieving compliance; parental respect for the child's autonomy; encouragement of independence, individuality, and responsibility; and relatively firm control and high demands for mature behavior. In short, authoritative parental practices—but not blind, authoritarian discipline—facilitate the development of mature personal and social behavior in children.

Family Interactions and Aggressive Behavior

Without intending to, family members may initiate and perpetuate children's undesirable and maladaptive behavior such as overaggressiveness. This was clearly documented in a series of studies of the antecedents and treatment of highly aggressive boys between the ages of 4 and 15 conducted by Gerald Patterson in Oregon.† The boys and their families became participants in the studies when they were referred to a clinic because they frequently displayed very high levels of aggressive behavior. They were defiant and negativistic, and they fought a great deal at home and at school. Control families, matched with the clinic population in age, socioeconomic status, and other important variables were also studied.

The aggressive boys' outbursts of aggression were, to a considerable degree, reactions to frustrations and punishments experienced in their own homes. Detailed observations confirmed that the aggressive child grows up in an aggressive atmosphere; all members of his family—parents and siblings—manifested more aggression than their counterparts in the control families. Members of the ag-

---

* D. Baumrind, "Socialization and Instrumental Competence in Young Children," in *The Young Child: Reviews of Research*, ed. W. W. Hartup (Washington, D.C.: National Association for the Education of Young Children, 1972), p. 217.

† G. R. Patterson, "Reprogramming the Families of Aggressive Boys," in *Behavior Modification in Education* (Yearbook of the National Society for the Study of Education), ed. C. E. Thoresen (Chicago: University of Chicago Press, 1972), pp. 154–94.

gressive child's family are prone to support "networks of maintaining stimuli"; that is, they stimulate and perpetuate each other's aggressive responses. For example, suppose a little girl teases her older brother; he responds by yelling at her because he has learned, from previous experiences, that this may stop her teasing. But if, on this occasion, the girl increases her teasing after her brother yells at her, his aggressive responses are likely to escalate. He may yell very loudly and swear, and if she then goes on teasing him, he may hit her and then repeat his hitting. This kind of incident of escalation of aggression was five times as frequent in the homes of the aggressive children as it was in the control families. Once started, an aggressive response is likely to be repeated several times within a very short period; aggressive children tend to have "bursts" of aggressive activity.

The disciplinary practices of the parents of aggressive children were markedly different from those used by the control parents. The reactions of the former to the child's aggressive expression were highly inconsistent: they sometimes rewarded hostile responses by approving, paying attention, complying with the child's wishes, and they sometimes punished these same responses severely by spanking. Often they would threaten punishment but fail to carry out their threats. When control parents threatened punishment for aggression, they ordinarily carried out their threats.

The investigators concluded that since the family's reactions stimulated and maintained the child's aggressive activity, altering the family's reaction patterns should result in reduction of the child's aggressive expression. They therefore designed a behavior modification program that the parents could implement, and the program proved to be very successful, as we shall see later.

Identification

As we have seen, many of the child's response patterns, characteristics, attitudes, and motives are acquired as a result of social learning and rewards at home. Other complicated reactions, behavior patterns, and motivational and emotional tendencies appear to be acquired spontaneously without direct training and without specific rewards. You may have observed nursery school girls whose posture, ways of moving, gestures, and speech inflections are duplicates of their mothers'. It is not likely that their mothers deliberately "taught" their daughters to emulate them in these ways or that they rewarded them directly for imitating their behaviors and mannerisms. In short, the mothers did not intend to teach these responses and the children did not intend to learn them. A more subtle process, *identification*, is involved.

Identification may be regarded as a *learned drive or motive to be similar to another individual*. When identifying with someone else, the child thinks, behaves, and feels as though the other person's characteristics were his or her own. Children are identifying with parents when they attempt to duplicate in their own lives the ideals, attitudes, and behavior of those parents. The person or group with whom the child identifies is referred to as the *model*, or *identificand*. How does identification seem to differ from observational learning? Identification undoubtedly involves observational learning; in fact, it may be reasonable to consider identification as a special type of observational learning, but it differs from simple imitation in several critical ways. First, identification may account for the adoption of a model's complex, integrated *patterns* of behavior, rather than the adoption of discrete responses. Second, identification responses are emitted spontaneously, without specific training or direct rewards. Two further characteristics differentiate identification from simple observational learning or imitation. Responses acquired through identification are generally relatively stable and enduring rather than transient. Finally, identification rests upon an intimate, personal relationship with the model, although children may emulate the responses of models whom they encounter only casually or briefly.

Identification is a fundamental mechanism of personality development and socialization. By identifying with parents, a child acquires many of their ways of behaving, thinking, and feeling. Moreover, since the parents are representatives of their culture, the child's identification with them provides skills, temperamental qualities, attitudes, motives, ideals, values, taboos, and morals appropriate for their cultural group. Through identification, as well as through learning by reward, the American middle-class child becomes competitive and achievement-oriented; the Hopi child becomes cooperative and democratic; Mundugamor children in New Guinea become harsh and aggressive; Japanese children become passive, accepting, and group-oriented.

Identification with the parent of the same sex helps the child to become appropriately sex-typed, that is, to incorporate characteristics and attitudes appropriate to the male or female role in his or her culture. As we have seen, the definitions of male and female behavior vary from culture to culture and may be modified considerably over time within a society. Nevertheless, in contemporary American society, as in most others, there are strong, prevalent pressures on boys to manifest characteristics defined as typically "masculine" and on girls to become "feminine." Yet many women have characteristics that were traditionally considered masculine—independence, self-assertion, and achievement orientation—and it appears that in the future there will be many more. If these women have daughters who identify with them, the girls will also adopt these characteristics.

In addition, through parental identification the child incorporates the culture's moral standards, values, and judgments. These are the components of what Freud labeled the *superego*, a mental structure that is formed through identification and functions as a kind of internalized monitor, judging the individual's behavior as good or bad, right or wrong. The superego punishes transgressions; after the superego develops, children punish themselves, largely through feelings of guilt and anxiety, whenever they do—or are tempted to do—something that is prohibited or immoral.

Identification begins early in life and is a prolonged—perhaps lifelong—process. As children mature, they continue to identify with their parents, acquiring more of their characteristics. As their social worlds expand, however, children find other identification models among their peers, teachers, ministers, and heroes from fiction, movies, and television, and they emulate their behaviors, characteristics, and ideals. In the end, the individual's personality will be based on a long series of identifications; some of the parents' characteristics will have been incorporated, and the behavior and ideas of a number of others will also be adopted. Since the child's personality is in large part derived from many different identifications, it will be complex and unique.

Erikson suggests that adolescence is the critical period for the integration and synthesis of past identifications, for dropping some and strengthening others. The adolescent faces an *identity crisis* that involves "finding oneself" and arriving at some satisfactory answer to the question, "Who am I?"

> The identity the adolescent seeks to clarify is who he is, what his role in society is to be: Is he a child or is he an adult? Does he have it in him to be someday a husband and father? What is he to be as a worker and an earner of money? Can he feel self-confident in spite of the fact that his race or religious or national background makes him a person some people look down upon? Overall, will he be a success or a failure? By reason of these questions adolescents are sometimes morbidly preoccupied with how they appear in the eyes of others as compared with their own conception of themselves.*

Earlier identifications and past learning and experience provide a foundation for a new and unique sense of *ego identity*, but "the

* Erikson, "Healthy Personality Development," p. 215.

whole has a different quality than the sum of the parts."* If they achieve substantial senses of ego identity, adolescents begin to regard themselves as individuals—self-consistent, integrated, unique persons worthy of the recognition of others. They are comfortable with themselves, know where they are going, and are not overly self-conscious or self-doubting. Failure to acquire a coherent sense of ego identity is called *ego diffusion*—the individuals have not "found themselves," are uncertain of their value as individuals, and lack a sense of purpose in life.

RESEARCH ON IDENTIFICATION   How is an identification with a model formed, and what are the underlying motivations? One hypothesis, based on social-learning theory, maintains that the motivation to identify with a model is rooted in the satisfactions derived from interactions with that model. Attractive, rewarding, strong, powerful, and nurturant models evoke more identification than models lacking these characteristics; the child is more apt to identify with a nurturant parent than with a rejecting one. A model who gratifies a child's needs becomes associated with feelings of satisfaction, pleasure, and comfort. The model as a person and his or her behavior and characteristics acquire reward value for the child. By identifying with this model, and thus incorporating the model's characteristics and behavior, the child becomes the source of his or her own rewards; children now react to themselves with the feelings of gratification that were originally associated with the model.

Support for this general hypothesis has been found in a number of investigations, In one study, two groups of mother-daughter pairs were the subjects. One group of mothers were judged to be nurturant (warm, giving, attentive, gratifying to the child), while the other group of mothers were judged not to be. Each mother was observed as she was teaching her daughter, a kindergarten pupil, to solve some maze problems. During the teaching session, each mother—the model in this situation—acting on instructions from the experimenter, performed a number of extraneous actions that had nothing to do with solving the problem. For example, she drew her lines very slowly, hesitated briefly at each choice point, made some unnecessary marks such as circles or loops in her tracing, and made some meaningless comments before each trial. The daughters of the nurturant mothers imitated many of these irrelevant, incidental behaviors, but the daughters of the nonnurturant mothers imitated very few. Thus, as the hypothesis predicted, mothers who were warm and gratifying elicited greater identification from their daughters—and more emulation of their behavior—than mothers who lacked these qualities.

* E. Erikson, "Identity and the Life Cycle," *Psychological Issues*, 1 (1959), 90.

In another relevant study, 40 boys age 5 were given a test of sex-role preferences (choosing among boys' and girls' toys and activities), and the 10 most masculine and 10 least masculine boys were selected for further study. It was assumed that high levels of masculine sex-typing were based on identification with their fathers, and that those low in sex-typing were only weakly identified with that parent. These 20 boys were seen in a doll-play session in which they used dolls representing a mother, father, and child to act out the endings of some incomplete stories. It is assumed that in describing the characters in the story, children reveal their self-perceptions and their feelings about their parents. As had been predicted, the responses of the highly masculine boys showed that they regarded their fathers as nurturant, warm, and rewarding, but the boys who were low in masculinity did not perceive their fathers in these ways.

Conscience Development

Since superego, or conscience, development is one of the major products of identification, we might expect morality in children to be related to identification and therefore to positive relationships with parents. And, indeed, there is evidence that this is the case, although it is extremely difficult to assess conscience development. One technique involves determining children's reactions to their own transgressions or wrongdoing. What does the child do if he or she breaks something, hits someone, or takes something without permission? Does the child feel guilty, confess, apologize, try to make restitution? Or does he or she lie, hide, and deny the wrongdoing?

The basic data of one study were mothers' reports of both parent-child relations and their children's reactions to their own transgressions. Analysis of the data showed that warm mothers tended to produce children who confessed their deviations, indicating guilt and strong conscience development. Boys who had accepting fathers also showed more guilt following wrongdoing and higher levels of conscience development than boys with rejecting fathers.

A high degree of conscience is promoted by the use of love-oriented disciplinary techniques, that is, techniques in which love is given or withheld to reward or to punish the child. Praise and reasoning as disciplinary techniques are associated with high conscience in children, whereas physical punishment is related to poor conscience development. The use of love-oriented disciplinary techniques is only effective for warm and loving mothers who maintain strong and affectionate relationships with their children. Children are in fact most likely to develop a high level of conscience if they have nurturant and affectionate mothers who threaten to withdraw love as punishment for disobedience. Conscience appears to be a consequence of an identification based on the child's fear of losing the love of an otherwise warm and loving parent.

Modeling and identification have significant effects on the development of various facets of moral behavior—such as generosity, altruism, and consideration—that are related to superego, or conscience. For example, in one study of generosity nursery school boys participated in a simple experiment, were rewarded with a number of trinkets for their participation, and were then given an opportunity to share their winnings with other children. Those who shared generously and those who shared very little or not at all were then observed in doll-play situations. The generous boys portrayed their fathers in doll play as warm, giving, nurturant, and affectionate; these kinds of father-perceptions were significantly less frequent among boys who were not generous.

Depth interviews with highly altruistic and self-sacrificing adults provide further evidence that identification is a significant factor underlying this behavior. Two types of volunteer workers were interviewed in depth during the civil rights movement of the 1960s. The *fully committed* civil rights workers in the 1960s made many personal sacrifices to participate in the movement, sometimes giving up their jobs and homes or postponing their education; the *partially committed* also worked in the movement but did not make such great personal sacrifices to do so. As youngsters and throughout adulthood, the *fully committed* were strongly identified with parents who were warm, nurturant, and themselves workers on behalf of justice, welfare, and human rights during their earlier years. As children, the fully committed were emotionally involved in their parents' socially oriented activities. This kind of identification was not apparent among the partially committed.

Other investigations show that parental disciplinary practices affect children's values and their consideration of others. A group of parents were interviewed or answered questionnaires about their reactions to their preadolescent children's misbehaviors. Their responses served as the basis for classifying their disciplinary techniques either as *power assertion* (controlling by physical power or material resources, including physical punishment, deprivation of privileges, threats) or as *induction* (which involves reasoning with the child, pointing out the painful consequences of his or her behavior for others). Those who employ induction predominantly as a disciplinary technique serve as models of consideration and demonstrate consideration of others (including their children), thus teaching their children to be considerate of the needs and feelings of others. Frequent use of induction by mothers was found to be related to high levels of consideration of others, as assessed by the children's peers (classmates were asked to nominate the children in the class who were most considerate of others). On the other hand, heavy use of power assertion was associated with low levels of children's consideration of others.

These findings were confirmed in other studies of preadolescents and their parents. Also, children of induction-using mothers ranked altruism very high among their personal values, while children of power-assertive mothers assigned high ranks to self-centered values such as earning a great deal of money and having a fine home and automobile

Juvenile delinquency may be regarded as a manifestation of deficient conscience development, a failure to incorporate or accept some of the culture's moral and ethical standards and prohibitions. This is a very complex problem; many factors are salient antecedents of delinquent behavior. Social and economic factors obviously play a major part, for delinquency rates are highest among the very poor and among disadvantaged minority and immigrant groups. These factors are not sufficient to produce delinquency, however; many children who grow up in poverty or have immigrant or minority parents do not become delinquent.

Studies conducted in different geographic areas and with different socioeconomic groups consistently show that delinquent behavior is related to failure to identify with parents and, consequently, to incorporate the culture's moral and ethical standards. Parents of delinquents, compared with those of nondelinquents of comparable intelligence and social status, are generally less affectionate, more indifferent, and more hostile toward them, and show less warmth and sympathy. Relatively few delinquents have close ties to their fathers, and many of them express open hostility toward both parents.

PEERS AS AGENTS OF SOCIALIZATION

During the first few years, children's social interactions are restricted largely to their own family circles, and their models for identification are parents and siblings. When they enter nursery school, their social world expands and increases in complexity and intensity. Peers become influential agents of socialization, "training" by reinforcing

certain responses and serving as models for imitation and identification. As a result, the young child's behavior, attitudes, and motivations may undergo major changes, although not all children are
equally affected by contacts with peers. Those who are shy and
withdrawn are less likely to have intensive interactions with other
children and are therefore less likely to be influenced by them.
Outgoing, explorative, relatively independent children are more
likely to participate in social activities and are consequently more
susceptible to influence. Popular nursery school children have a
broader range of social contacts, give others more rewards, and are
more often the targets of rewards; they are more likely to influence
their peers and in turn be influenced by them.

From an adult point of view, some of the changes resulting
from interactions with peers are desirable, others undesirable. Nursery school children's sex-typed responses and characteristics are apt
to become strengthened and more firmly entrenched as the result of
peers' reinforcement of sex-stereotyped patterns of behavior and their
punishment of sex-inappropriate responses. Nursery school boys reward other boys for traditionally masculine behavior such as playing
with trucks and guns; girls reinforce one another for traditionally
feminine activities such as playing with dolls. In some cases, peer
influences may counteract the effects of training and identification in
the home. For example, a young boy who is highly identified with
his mother may have acquired many characteristics that his peers
consider "feminine." After associating with other boys at the nursery
school, however, his behavior may shift substantially in a more
"masculine" direction. Kindness, cooperation, and friendliness are
likely to bring rewards from peers and hence are likely to be repeated and strengthened. Some behaviors bring peer disapproval and
punishment—selfishness, dependency, and babyishness, for example—and these responses are likely to be weakened or eliminated
(extinguished).

Aggressive responses, such as attacking others and attempting
to seize another's toys or invade another child's "territory," are often
rewarded in nursery school and thus strengthened. Children who
have already established highly aggressive patterns of behavior are
likely to become even more aggressive when they attend nursery
school because other children may reward their aggressiveness by
yielding to the aggressors' wishes or withdrawing from conflict. In addition, children who are relatively unaggressive initially are also
likely to become more aggressive. While they may be frequent targets
of aggression at first, many such children eventually counterattack
and refuse to give up things they want to keep. Their new assertive
and aggressive reactions are likely to be successful sometimes and

hence to become stronger and more frequent. Some children are initially unaggressive and at the same time very passive and socially withdrawn; these children are not likely to counterattack when they are the targets of aggression and hence are not rewarded for aggressive behavior. These children are not likely to become more aggressive in nursery school.

Peers as Models

Nursery school children readily identify with other children and spontaneously imitate their peers' actions, both desirable and undesirable. Those who are at first mild-mannered are likely to become more assertive if they observe their playmates using force and threats to attain goals. Children will readily imitate the aggressive patterns of other children—striking others, screaming, kicking, destroying things. If they observe these repeatedly, they may adopt them as their own habitual responses, especially if they are successful in obtaining goals.

Analogously, children are likely to copy their peers' prosocial reactions, including donating to charity, expressing sympathy, or helping someone in distress. Repeated exposure to prosocial peer models may produce strong, enduring, and generalized altruistic dispositions in the same way that repeated exposure to adult models does. If kindergarten children play with others who are socially more mature, they themselves become more cooperative, participate in more group activities, and more often use requests and suggestions rather than force in dealing with others. And, as one experiment showed, children's generosity (sharing prizes they win) increased after they observed peer models behaving altruistically; control subjects, who did not observe generous models, were not nearly as generous in sharing.

As the child grows older and spends more time away from home, peers become more influential as teachers and models. School children conform more to the norms and standards of the peer group than younger children do. In middle childhood, the peer group can be very helpful in training the child to adapt to the broader social world, to interact with larger groups, and to relate to leaders. Peers can also provide guidance and assistance in achieving better personal adjustment, teaching the child new and effective ways of dealing with complex feelings—hostility, dominance, dependence, and independence. Discussion with peers and sharing problems, conflicts, and complex feelings may be reassuring; the discovery that other children are also angry with their parents or are concerned with masturbation may help relieve tension and guilt. Children's feelings about school, as well as their academic interests, aims, and aspirations, may be strongly influenced by their peers' attitudes toward education. The development of the child's self-concept is also affected directly and indirectly by interactions with peers. Acceptance by peers is likely to augment self-confidence, while general rejection may lower self-esteem.

In contemporary American culture, the peer group is more influential than in most other societies. Children reared in traditional China or in Mexican villages, as well as in rural or small town America in earlier times, were much more oriented toward their families and much less concerned with the peer group's attitudes, standards, and behaviors. In some other societies, such as in Israeli kibbutzim and in the Soviet Union, children are as much or more concerned with peer approval as with their families' reactions. Urie Bronfenbrenner, an authority on child rearing in the Soviet Union, maintains that peers in that country are more powerful socializers than parents. The values of the adult social and political systems have been very well inculcated in Soviet children, however; conforming to peer pressure therefore serves to maintain these systems.

Peer-Group Influences during Adolescence

For many reasons, peer influences appear to be greatest during adolescence. Adolescents are marginal persons—no longer children, not yet adults—and there are many pressures on them. Within a relatively short period of time they must make numerous adjustments. They must gradually achieve independence from their families; adjust to sexual maturity; establish cooperative, workable relationships with peers; decide on and prepare for a vocation; develop some kind of philosophy of life or a set of guiding moral beliefs and standards; and develop a sense of identity. At the same time, ties to parents weaken progressively as independence is achieved.

Under the circumstances, it is not difficult to understand why adolescents are likely to feel close to others who have the same problems, who can help them gain clearer concepts of themselves, their problems, and their goals. Peers may be more successful than parents in giving the adolescent a feeling of personal worth and realistic perspectives and hopes for the future. The culture has changed extremely rapidly and in many ways since the parents of today's adolescents were themselves adolescents. There are new and different pressures to adjust to. Furthermore, watching their adolescent children trying to cope with problems, parents may find their own adolescent feelings and conflicts reawakened, and this may be extremely uncomfortable. For these reasons, parents often have great difficulties in communicating with their adolescent children and in understanding and sharing their problems, even though they make sincere efforts to do so. Understandably, they worry about the "generation gap."

All of these factors heighten the significance of peer groups during adolescence, and therefore there is strong motivation to conform to peer-culture values, customs, and fads during this period. Yet it would be a mistake to infer that conformity to peer-group standards inevitably implies diminished parental influence for most adolescents. For one thing, there is usually considerable overlap between parental and peer values because the child's friends are likely to come from the same background. The friends of a white Protestant middle-class adolescent are likely to come from that same group. Furthermore,

> neither parental nor peer influence is monolithic. The weight given to either [parent or peer opinion] will depend to a significant degree on the adolescent's appraisal of its relative value in a specific situation. For example, peer influence is more likely to be predominant in such matters as tastes in music and entertainment, fashions in clothing and language, patterns of same- and opposite-sex peer interaction, and the like; while parental influence is more likely to be predominant in such areas as underlying moral and social values and understanding of the adult world.*

Adolescents are most likely to become very strongly identified with their peer group if their parents fail to provide adequate nurturance and support, that is, if they do not foster strong parental identification. Parental influence is more powerful than peer influence among adolescents whose parents express affection, interest, understanding, and willingness to be helpful. In contrast, according to the data of one study, strongly peer-oriented adolescents rate their parents low in affection, support, and control. In brief,

> the peer-oriented child is more a product of parental disregard than of the attractiveness of the peer group . . . he turns to his age-mates less by choice than by default. The vacuum left by the withdrawal of parents and adults from the lives of children is filled with . . . the substitute of an age-segregated peer group.†

After an exhaustive review of the relevant literature, one authority on adolescent adjustment concluded that a marked decline

---

* J. J. Conger, "A World They Never Knew: The Family and Social Change," *Daedalus*, 100, no. 4 (1971), 1128, 1129.

† Ibid., p. 1129.

in parental influence, accompanied by increase in peer influence, is most likely to occur where

> (1) there is a very strong, homogeneous peer group with patterns of behavior and attitudes that differ markedly from those of parents; (2) a rewarding parent-child relationship is lacking at the outset, due to a lack of parental interest and understanding, manifest willingness to be helpful, and shared family activities; (3) the parents' own values and behaviors are inconsistent, uninformed, unrealistic, maladaptive, or obviously hypocritical; (4) the adolescent lacks either the self-confidence (based on a positive self-image) or the independence training to act autonomously without undue concern; or (5) as it is phrased on multiple-choice examinations, "all of the above." In most cases where young people have forsaken or renounced family values for those of deviant peer groups, one or more of these conditions is likely to obtain.*

STABILITY
OF PERSONALITY CHARACTERISTICS

There would be little interest in investigating the antecedents of children's personality characteristics if these characteristics were ephemeral, transient, or highly subject to change. The question of stability or continuity of early-established personality traits is a critical one. If we know what the child is like at 4, for example, can we predict what he or she will be like in the future—at age 5 or 8, at adolescence, or in adulthood?

The answer is a qualified affirmative. Many personality characteristics established early in life appear to be stable and enduring; if we know the child's status with respect to certain dimensions of personality—such as introversion, aggression, dependency, general adjustment—we can predict his or her later standing in these dimensions reasonably well. Adult maladjustment, for example, is often an extension of early-established maladjustments; most emotionally disturbed adults suffered intense conflicts, feelings of rejection, and inadequacy during childhood.

Longitudinal studies offer unique opportunities to investigate the persistence of personality characteristics from childhood to adulthood in normal (nonclinical) populations. A number of these studies show that the dimension of extroversion—or its opposite, introversion—is established very early in life and tends to remain highly stable. In one study, 5-year-olds who were anxious in social situations were also likely to be shy when they were adolescents,

* Ibid., p. 1130.

and children who were inhibited and apprehensive in their relationships with others in early childhood (ages 6 to 10) became tense adults who were uncomfortable in social situations.

Another longitudinal study showed that 4-year-olds who received high ratings from their nursery school teachers in generosity, helpfulness, cooperation, and consideration also responded generously to an opportunity to help another child a year later. Social responsibility and altruism are also relatively stable characteristics during childhood. In one study, children were observed in nursery school and again five or six years later when they were in elementary school. Those who were socially responsible and altruistic at the earlier period also behaved in these ways at the later period.

The participants in the Fels longitudinal study, 71 predominantly middle-class people, were studied from birth through early adulthood.* Their parents were interviewed and the subjects themselves frequently tested and observed in their homes, nursery schools, day camps, and schools. Personality characteristics such as dependency, passivity, aggression, and achievement motivation were rated at five age periods: 0–3, 3–6, 6–10, 10–14, and young adulthood (20–29). The ratings for the four childhood periods were made by a psychologist who had no knowledge of the adult subjects' personalities; another psychologist, working independently and knowing nothing about the subjects' early development, interviewed them in depth when they were adults and then rated them on the same variables.

A substantial number of personality characteristics remained stable from childhood through adolescence and adulthood. Motivation to achieve, especially in intellectual tasks, begins to stabilize in the age period from 3 to 6 and becomes increasingly stable between 6 and 10 years. Children who showed interest in mastering intellectual skills during the preschool period were likely to be highly motivated for intellectual achievement during elementary school and during adolescence and adulthood. Children who were inhibited and apprehensive in their relationships with others in early childhood (ages 6 to 10) became tense adults who were uncomfortable in social situations.

Characteristics that have been traditionally sex-typed also showed stability. For example, boys in our culture are generally more aggressive than girls, while girls are more dependent. Measures of aggression were consistently more stable for boys than for girls. Boys who had temper tantrums and displayed rage in the early years

* J. Kagan and H. Moss, *Birth to Maturity* (New York: John Wiley & Sons, 1969).

of elementary school became easily angered adolescents and later, as adults, were very prone to be verbally aggressive when frustrated. In contrast, dependency and passivity were more stable for girls than for boys. Girls who were highly dependent on others and reacted passively to frustrations during early childhood became passive adolescents, closely tied to their families, and as young women, they relied on others to help them solve their problems. Relatively independent adolescent girls were likely to grow into independent and self-sufficient adults.

While some of this evidence is impressive, we must be cautious not to overgeneralize the findings. For one thing, there is little evidence of stability of many characteristics observed in the *very* early periods of life. The results of one longitudinal study suggest that "emotional adjustment as reflected by happy, calm, and positive behavior during the child's first two years may not be predictive of later overt behavior."* Most of the stable traits discussed above began to stabilize during the period from 6 to 10 years; very few stabilized during the preschool period.

Furthermore, correlations between early and later behavior, though positive and significant, are far from perfect. This means that many people *do* change in characteristics such as achievement motivation, aggression, and dependency, although for the population at large these traits are well formed in early childhood and persist through later periods. But there is little reason to believe that personality development ends in early childhood; rather, it seems that many important aspects of personality remain open to change over long spans of time. Clinical psychologists who have studied people longitudinally over long periods have found that many maladjusted or neurotic children—presumably "high risks" for subsequent maladjustment—somehow overcome their difficulties and become well-adjusted, well-functioning adults. Others who are relatively well adjusted as youngsters somehow become anxious or neurotic adults.

SITUATIONAL DETERMINANTS OF BEHAVIOR

Situational factors—stimuli in the immediate environment, especially social ones—also exert powerful influences on behavior, and sometimes they are the prepotent determinants of actions. Whatever

* E. S. Schaefer and N. Bayley, *Maternal Behavior, Child Behavior, and Their Intercorrelations from Infancy Through Adolescence*, Monographs of the Society for Research in Child Development, 28, no. 3 (whole no. 87) (1963), 48.

their personality structure, Americans drive on the right-hand side of the road, except under very unusual conditions. Whether dependent or independent, assertive or unassertive, introverted or extroverted, Americans do not laugh during religious services, funeral orations, or recitations of marriage vows. The cultural rules for behavior in these settings are set and inflexible; hardly anyone deviates from the standard, culturally prescribed behavior.

For the vast majority of situations that the individual encounters, the rules for behavior are not so rigid, however. In most situations, the child's behavior is a function of *both* personality characteristics and the immediate environmental conditions. To illustrate, let us look at behavior in a crisis. If a child is basically secure and calm, his or her behavior ordinarily reflects these characteristics. But faced with an event such as fire, storm, or injury the child may display fear or panic. Children who are generally anxious, fearful, and excitable may react even more strongly. To cite a less extreme example, a youngster may be anxious, dependent, and aggressive when with tense and punitive parents but may be calm and independent in a relaxed and friendly nursery school atmosphere.

Frustration and Aggression

Everyone occasionally encounters a frustration—an obstacle interfering with the achievement of a desired goal. Frustration may be regarded as a *situational* variable, and reactions to it have been studied extensively, in both experimental and natural settings. One of the most common reactions is aggression. In nursery school, aggressive conflicts between children are likely to increase when the amount of play space is limited and when, consequently, there are more frustrations and interferences.

Children subjected to experimentally produced frustrations are likely to react with aggressive responses, especially if they are in a permissive situation where aggression does not lead to punishment. In one study, preschool boys and girls were observed playing with dolls for two 30-minute sessions. During the first, they were allowed to play freely. But before the second session, one group of subjects, the *failure* or *frustration group*, worked at extremely difficult tasks that made them feel unsuccessful and frustrated. The *control group* was not experimentally frustrated before the second doll-play session.

In the second session, both groups displayed more aggression than they had during the first play period, probably because the permissive atmosphere permitted such expression. The frustration group, however, showed significantly *greater increases in aggression* than the control group. Apparently, the experience of frustration elicited the subsequent heightened aggressiveness.

In a sense, frustration, like beauty, is in the eye of the beholder. The child's *interpretation* of a frustrating situation, rather than any absolute amount of frustration, is most relevant in determining his or her reactions, and this interpretation may be affected by situational factors. If a child's toy is broken by another child, the victim will react with greater hostility if he or she interprets the other's action as intentional rather than accidental. In one experiment, children in the third grade were frustrated by a somewhat older child who was an accomplice (confederate) of the experimenter. The frustrator prevented the subjects from completing some simple block-construction tasks and thus from earning some money. Following the frustration, some of the children were told that the frustrator was tired and upset, that under other conditions he would have been more cooperative. The remainder of the frustrated children, in control groups, were not given these explanations of the extenuating circumstances. Shortly afterward, each subject met the frustrator in another setting and had an opportunity to interfere with or help him. The group that had been told of the frustrator's problems showed significantly less aggression toward him than the control children. In effect, frustration in the "interpretation" group had been reduced, and consequently aggressive expression was also reduced.

The amount of frustration and the perception or interpretation of the frustration are not the only determinants of the intensity of aggressive reactions. Some children become violently aggressive in response to a relatively minor frustration, while others hardly become aggressive at all under the same frustrating circumstances. Why? Because from past experience, some children acquire higher degrees of "tolerance," a marked ability to endure frustration without becoming upset. Preschool children who according to tests have developed such tolerance display significantly less aggression than children in the same nursery school who experience the same frustrations but have lower tolerances.

Moreover, children differ in the intensity of their acquired fears of punishment for aggressiveness. Among boys studied at one juvenile correctional institution, those with strong fears of punishment were less aggressive than their peers who were relatively unafraid, even though the two groups were in the same situation (the institution) and experienced the same frustrations. Apparently, then, the intensity of a child's aggression is a function not only of the situation—although that is important—but also of the personality structure he or she has developed.

EFFECTS OF WATCHING TELEVISION   Violence has become an increasingly prominent subject of the mass media in recent years. The question of whether exposure to violence leads to greater aggression in children inevitably arises. Specifically, is the violence observed in movies and on television likely to augment a child's aggressive tendencies? The general public and governmental concern with the possible detrimental effects of television on children seems justified, since commercial television contains an enormous amount of murder, fighting, and brutality. It is estimated that about 70 percent of television programs contain at least one incident of violence.

The issue has been investigated repeatedly in experimental studies in which subjects are shown films portraying aggressive interactions; control groups are exposed to films of the same length that have no violent content. Following this, the children are given an opportunity to behave aggressively, and those who were exposed to the aggressive films almost invariably show more aggression than the control groups. This experimental finding has been replicated in many studies. Even after a single exposure to violent cartoons, children manifest higher levels of aggressive behavior toward peers than controls do, although the effects are generally short-lived. Repeated exposure has more significant and lasting effects, however, and these are particularly marked in the case of children with strong aggressive tendencies—that is, those who are habitually highly aggressive. Heavy viewers of violence not only behave more aggressively, but they also have positive attitudes toward aggression, regarding it as an effective way to deal with conflicts.

Frequent viewing of violent television programs may also have cumulative, long-term effects on aggressive expression. This was the finding of a longitudinal study in which children's television preferences were ascertained when they were in the third grade; their aggression was also assessed 10 years later, when they were freshmen in college. Compared with their peers, boys with strong preferences for violent programs when they were youngsters were more aggressive as young adults.

In spite of the fact that the findings are consistent in showing that exposure to television violence is likely to lead to increased aggression by child viewers, we must be cautious about interpretation and overgeneralization. After all, most of the studies are laboratory studies, conducted in artificial environments quite different from the settings in which children ordinarily watch television. Furthermore, limited measures of aggression are used in many studies, and it is not known whether these give valid indications of aggression in other situations. There is an urgent need for better data on the effects of television violence on a wide range of children's responses in real-life situations. It is clear that television violence is not beneficial to child viewers; nevertheless, we must be cautious about making television the scapegoat for the high levels of violence in our society.

Situational Determinants of Dependency

While the strength of a child's dependency needs is to a large extent a consequence of early relationships with family and peers, manifestations of dependency are also strongly influenced by the immediate situation. Infants who are away from their mothers for short periods show intense attachment behavior when they are re-united—clinging to the mother and refusing to be put down, crying whenever she leaves, and showing intense fear when approached by strangers. If a mother temporarily provides less nurturance than usual, she may expect her baby to manifest more than the usual degree of dependent behavior.

The effects on dependency of "social deprivation"—isolation from social contacts or a reduction in the normal level of social interaction—have been studied extensively. For example, in one experimental study each preschool subject played alone, without any social interaction, for 20 minutes before participating in a simple learning experiment. A control group of children was presented with the same learning problem but did not experience this kind of social deprivation. The reward for correct responses during learning was a social one: verbal approval by the experimenter.

The experimental (deprived) subjects were more responsive to this reward; that is, they learned faster than the control group did. Apparently, absence of social interaction—and the concomitant lack of gratification of dependency needs—leads to a greater need for attention and approval (dependence on others), thus increasing the reward value of verbal expressions of approval. Furthermore, children who are characteristically more dependent (according to observation of their behavior in nursery school) reacted more favorably to adult approval in the experimental situation.

Another experimental study demonstrates even more clearly that deprivation of social contact and reassurance heightens a child's dependency. A female experimenter, while watching a group of nursery school children playing freely with toys, gave them a great deal of attention and affection, thus gratifying their dependency needs. Then, abruptly, she stopped talking to them, withdrawing her attention and nurturance and refusing to answer their questions. In psychological terms, after gratifying the children's dependency needs for a period of time, she frustrated them. A control group of children received consistent dependency-need gratification; that is, the experimenter did not withdraw her affection and attention or frustrate their dependency needs. Later, while learning a task, the children in the frustrated group appeared to be much more highly motivated to seek praise by the experimenter—that is, to be nurtured and to have their dependency needs gratified—than the control group. Apparently, gratification of dependency needs, when followed by social deprivation, amplified their dependency motivation. This was particularly true for the girls.

As in the study reported above, boys who were ordinarily highly dependent reacted most strongly to this frustration; they became highly motivated to receive praise from the experimenter. Independent boys, however, were not so much affected by withdrawal of nurturance and attention. We may conclude that although deprivation of nurturance and warmth is likely to strengthen a young child's dependency needs at least temporarily, the intensity of the child's reactions is conditioned by his or her personality structure and earlier experiences.

Moods and Prosocial Behavior

Transient moods, including feelings of success and failure, are situational variables that have substantial effects on both children's and adults' behavior. Failure to achieve something one wants is, of course, a frustration; the feeling of failure may lead to greater proneness to react quickly and vigorously to other frustrations. Furthermore, transient moods affect the probability of acting prosocially. People more readily assist others and share possessions when they feel happy, pleased, or successful in some undertaking. Feelings of failure and sadness tend to reduce children's sharing and cooperation.

THE MODIFICATION
OF CHILDREN'S PERSONALITY CHARACTERISTICS

The fact that children's behavior can be influenced significantly by situational factors is further evidence that the behavior patterns of young children are flexible and modifiable. Consequently, if they encounter new situations, particularly new social interactions, their personality structures and behaviors may undergo radical modifications.

To illustrate, experiences with peers in school may foster self-confidence in a child who previously lacked this characteristic. A shy, sullen, and withdrawn child, the product of a harsh and restrictive home environment, may expand in a permissive nursery school with warm, understanding teachers, becoming lively, happy, and creative. Similarly, a boy who is unable to identify with a cold, unkind father may be retarded in the acquisition of sex-typed characteristics and interests. If he forms a strong friendship with a highly masculine boy, identification may then promote and accelerate the boy's sex-typing, compensating at least in part for earlier difficulties in this area.

On the other hand, unfortunate school or neighborhood experiences may undermine the beneficial effects of good parent-child relationships. For example, if parents have been warm, gentle, and permissive, children may enter school feeling secure, self-possessed, and confident. But if they are below average in intelligence or lacking in motivation to study, they may experience crushing failures in school and as a consequence become frustrated and aggressive. They may change from socially outgoing and pleasant youngsters into unhappy, withdrawn, and socially maladjusted ones. In short, encountering new situations—particularly social relationships—may lead to major readjustments and significant alterations in children's personality and behavior.

Simple applications of basic principles of social learning and reinforcement may produce dramatic modifications in behavior and personality characteristics. In one classic experiment, 12 nursery school children with immature reactions to failure (retreating, giving up easily, crying, sulking) were given special training designed to increase their perseverance and independence in solving difficult problems. A control group of 12 children who were only slightly immature received no special training. In the training, the experimenter met with each of the children a number of times, introducing them to problems and encouraging them to work the problems out independently. As training progressed, the problems became more complex and difficult, but the youngsters became more interested and gained continuously in independence. They requested less help and persevered longer in their attempts to solve the problems. Spontaneous comments showing self-confidence (for instance, "It's a hard problem but I'm getting better all the time") became more frequent.

After training, the control and experimental groups were given new, difficult puzzles to solve. The trained group showed a significantly greater increase in independence than the controls and greater interest than they had shown originally, and they worked harder than they had before training. Crying, sulking, aggressive outbursts, and destruction occurred less frequently as reactions to difficult problems. Mature, independent responses, learned during the training, were apparently generalized to the new problems. Those in the control group, however, did not show significant improvements in their attempts to solve difficult problems or in their reactions to frustration.

Nursery school teachers can create simple new situations that produce some behavior modifications. As we have seen, some children behave very aggressively in the permissive milieu of the nursery school. Nevertheless, slight changes in the teachers' responses to aggression may produce some marked modifications in aggression, as the following study demonstrated. For two weeks the experimenters, who were teachers in a nursery school, ignored children's aggression as much as possible and rewarded cooperative and peaceful behavior with attention and praise. Pupils' aggressive responses had been observed and rated for a week before the training period to determine their "base rate," and similar ratings were made again after the first week of the training period.

The simple manipulations of rewarding cooperation and ignoring (not rewarding) aggression were remarkably successful very quickly, and apparently had some enduring effects. Acts of physical and verbal aggression decreased significantly in the second week of the experiment, while the number of cooperative acts increased. Some extremely aggressive boys became friendly and cooperative to a degree that could hardly have been anticipated before the training began. The source of these impressive changes was a simple manipulation of the environment, a straightforward application of basic principles of reinforcement learning.

Parents can readily learn basic principles of behavior modification and apply them successfully in changing some aspects of their children's behavior. Since boys' highly aggressive behaviors are perpetuated by the reactions of members of their families, Patterson and his colleagues devised a behavior modification program that parents could use to reduce a child's aggression.* The parents were first trained to define and keep accurate records of certain "target" behaviors, the most undesirable of their children's aggressive responses. Then, through modeling and role-playing, they were taught effective ways of rewarding desirable responses and ignoring or punishing aggressive acts. Application of these techniques proved to be very successful in "shaping" their sons' behaviors. After a few months of the treatment program, over 75 percent of the aggressive boys showed major reductions in the amount of aggression expressed and

* Patterson, "Reprogramming the Families of Aggressive Boys," pp. 154–94.

the number of "bursts" of aggressive behavior. No such change had occurred in a matched control group of aggressive boys and their families. Apparently, parents can control their children's aggression simply by applying principles of "good parenting," together with a consistent program of rewards and punishments.

Peers may also be agents of behavior modification (and successful psychotherapists!) simply by modeling adaptive behavior. This was dramatically illustrated in the study of the "treatment" of a group of children of nursery school age who had dog phobias (excessive fear of dogs). On eight occasions, they observed a 4-year-old model playing with a dog and petting him. In each successive session, the model stayed with the dog for a longer period of time, interacting with him more intensively. A control group of children with equally severe phobias did not observe the model. The day after the treatment series was completed, each child was observed as he or she encountered the dog again. Those who had observed the model approached the dog readily, petted him, and played with him. A month later these gains were still apparent, and friendly approach responses were generalized from the familiar dog to an unfamiliar one. The controls, however, were just as fearful as they had been previously and avoided the dog.

Films of peer models can also be effective in decreasing timidity and promoting sociability. Some withdrawn nursery school children were exposed to films of peers watching other children at play and then joining the activities and enjoying participation. After viewing this film, the children became much more sociable in nursery school and engaged in many more peer interactions than they had previously. A control group did not see the film; they did not become less withdrawn and continued to avoid social relationships with their peers. The intervention had lasting effects. A month later those who were exposed to the film continued to find interactions with other children very enjoyable.

Experiments and observations such as these lead us to conclude that a young child's immature and maladaptive responses can be modified relatively readily. With fairly simple training, a child may acquire better ways of coping with frustration and become more independent, more persevering, calmer, less aggressive, more cooperative, more sociable, and less fearful. Most significantly, the new responses in the training situation are likely to generalize to other situations.

The Development
of Social Behavior

Our discussion of personality development in chapters 4 and 5 necessarily included some consideration of significant aspects of social behavior, because evaluations of children's personality are based largely on observations of their interactions with others. For example, we judge children to be highly aggressive if they attack or quarrel with peers frequently, altruistic if they do things for others, and dependent if they seek a great deal of aid or reassurance. Thus, the reader already has some knowledge about the development of social interactions and the antecedents of individual differences in social behavior. In the present chapter our attention will be centered directly on the nature and characteristics of peer interactions, including friendship; on the structure of children's groups; on peer acceptance or popularity; on leadership; and on children's values, opinions and attitudes.

Psychologists can study children's social behavior and development by means of careful, naturalistic observation or by using experimental methods. In *observation*, an investigator usually finds a good lookout station in a nursery school, playground, or meeting place and, usually using a time-sampling method, systematically records children's interactions. For example, a researcher interested in aggressive behavior would note all instances of hitting, destroying toys, and shouting at the teacher or other children. Or a checklist with many aggression items might be used, and appropriate behaviors would be recorded as they occurred. In *experiments* on the development of social behavior, children are observed in specially contrived settings, and their reactions to the situation and to other children are recorded.

SOCIAL BEHAVIOR
DURING THE PRESCHOOL YEARS

Babies become responsive to social stimulation, particularly by their caretakers, very early. But it is difficult to determine exactly wheɪ they begin to react socially to their peers. If infants between 6 and 12 months of age are placed near each other, they look at, approach, and explore each other, and a little later, toward the end of the first year, some will share toys. These contacts are very brief, ranging from a few seconds to a minute, and most of them are not real social interactions; rather, one child initiates a social contact but generally elicits no response beyond a gaze or glance from the others. In one study, babies in the second year of life were brought together in groups with their mothers present in the room. They interacted in more varied and complicated ways than younger babies—approaching and attempting to make contact, pinching, squeezing, disputing, offering things to each other, hitting, attracting another child's attention; most social contacts lasted less than 30 seconds, however, and there was very little interactive play. If babies this age are put together in pairs—in a playpen, for example—they are much more responsive to each other. Displays of sociability increase with age in the first two years. The participants in one study, babies between 6 and 25 months of age, were placed together in pairs in a playpen and observed for four-minute periods. With increasing age, responses changed steadily from initial indifference toward the partner to social interest and cooperative play. Infants between 6 and 8 months of age generally ignored each other, but there were a few rudimentary social contacts, such as looking, smiling, and grasping the partner. Babies between 9 and 13 months of age paid some attention to their partners, and conflicts occurred if one child attempted to snatch a toy from the other. Between 14 and 18 months, attention to the partner as an individual increased considerably, and conflicts over toys simultaneously decreased. Between 19 and 25 months, the number of social contacts—looking and smiling at the partner—increased, and play became far more cooperative and friendly. In general, for children in the second year, being in a confined area with one other child is more conducive to sociability than is a situation that includes many babies together in a large room. Even under the best circumstances, however, social relationships during the second year are limited.

By the age of 2 many babies seem to prefer to interact with other children than to play by themselves. Children of this age imitate each other's actions, direct smiles toward each other, vocalize, offer and exchange toys, or play social games. They occasionally have direct conflicts—for example, if both are attracted to the same toy.

With increasing age during the nursery school period, interactions increase in frequency, intensity, and duration. Children spend more time in cooperative activities (playing with others in joint projects, sharing materials) and less time sitting idly, playing alone, or simply watching others. By nursery school age, children seem to feel emotionally secure when with familiar peers, even if their mothers are not present, and they seek peers' attention and praise. As they grow older, children's social interactions last longer and are more enjoyable; strong attachments to friends are established.

According to the data of one longitudinal study of social interactions, by the age of 3, children have acquired relatively stable ways of relating to others their own age. Some interact primarily by dispute, assault, and protest, while others have more positive approaches to their peers, giving them things, cooperating in work and play, and expressing affection.

These age changes in social behavior may be attributable in part to the fact that nursery school offers many opportunities for interactions with peers. Also, children's increased physical and cognitive skills permit participation in more complex cooperative activities. Parents and teachers generally encourage children this age to engage in social activities; in addition, peers reward the children's outgoing and friendly responses at nursery school and on the playground. Consequently, these responses are more apt to be repeated. At the same time, inactivity, solitary play and nonparticipation are discouraged by parents and nursery school teachers, so that these responses tend to become weaker and diminish.

Preschool Friendships

Between the ages of 2 and 5, the number of conflicts and quarrels between children decreases steadily and friendly contacts become more prominent. During these years, children form their first friendships, usually with others of their own sex, although sex cleavage in social relationships is not as strong at this age as during middle childhood and preadolescence. Between the ages of 2 and 3, the number of friends a child has tends to increase; after this age, closer attachments to a few particular friends develop. Nevertheless, preschool friendships are generally casual, unstable, and highly transient.

A socially oriented and responsive preschooler who seeks out companions has a variety of social experiences, some satisfying and some frustrating. Consequently, he or she may exhibit social responses that seem contradictory. For example, preschool friends tend to argue more frequently with each other than children who rarely associate with one another. Many highly aggressive nursery school children are also very sympathetic with their classmates, responding readily to their distress. The child who grabs a toy from a playmate at one moment may rush to comfort a crying, unhappy child the next.

Popularity during Preschool

Popular children and leaders can be distinguished as early as the nursery school period. Some children are continually being sought out as playmates; others are consistently shunned and avoided by their nursery school classmates. The popularity status of a child can be assessed by observing his or her social participation directly, noting the number and nature of social contacts with peers. Or *sociometric* questions can be used; children are asked to name (or to choose from among the pictures of all the children in the school) the children in their class they like best, want to play with, want to sit next to, dislike, and so forth.

Popularity has been found to be significantly correlated with behavioral measures of friendliness (number of friendly approaches to others and participation in associative play). Compared with unpopular children, popular children give their peers more social reinforcements (attention or approval, affection, indications of acceptance, imitation of another child, willing compliance with another's request), and they give these reinforcements to a greater number of children. Aggressiveness is negatively correlated with popularity; popular children have relatively few fights with others, and they seldom attack or insult their peers. They also tend to be generally conforming and cooperative in their approach to nursery school routines, not because they are passive or overly compliant but rather because they are willing "to modulate their own behavior and to make necessary compromises toward the peaceful and efficient operation of the group."*

* S. G. Moore, "Correlates of Peer Acceptance in Nursery School Children," in *The Young Child: Reviews of Research*, ed. W. W. Hartup and N. L. Smothergil (Washington, D.C.: National Association for the Education of Young Children, 1967), p. 241.

Dependency is also related to peer acceptance but in rather complicated ways. Emotional dependence on adults—for example, seeking attention, comfort, and support from teachers—is significantly negatively related to popularity. Peer-oriented dependency, on the other hand, is positively correlated. "A child's need or desire to seek help, affection, and support from his companions may actually enhance him in their eyes. Young children may be somewhat flattered at having a companion come to them for help, affection, and support."*

Social Conflicts

There are great individual differences in proneness to conflicts, but the average nursery school child between 2 and 4 years of age is involved in some sort of conflict every five minutes. Boys tend to participate in more conflicts and make more attacks, whereas girls tend to argue more. These sex differences are more pronounced among older nursery school children, reflecting their more firmly established sex-typing of behavior.

In general, the interactions of preschool youngsters are more characteristically cooperative and friendly than unfriendly, hostile, or competitive. Even the most highly aggressive preschool children actually make more friendly responses than aggressive ones. Aggressiveness, incidentally, tends to be a fairly stable characteristic; the frequency of a child's conflicts during nursery school is a reliable indicator of his or her proneness to conflict in kindergarten.

SOCIAL RELATIONSHIPS
IN MIDDLE CHILDHOOD

Social relationships during the school years are more extensive, more intense, and more important to the child than those of the earlier years. While preschool friendships are generally casual and of short duration, the schoolchild's friends are likely to be important agents of socialization, having direct and powerful impacts on his or her personality and social development.

From roughly ages 7 to 12, youngsters are strongly concerned with their "gang," an informal group with a fairly rapid turnover in membership. Later on, between the ages of 10 and 14, more highly structured groups with formal organization and membership require-

*Ibid., p. 244.

ments, such as Boy Scouts and Girl Scouts, become more salient, especially among middle-class children.

Popularity

The personality characteristics associated with popularity during middle childhood parallel those associated with preschool popularity—friendliness, sociability, outgoingness, sensitivity to the needs and feelings of other children, and enthusiasm. Good-looking boys and girls are popular with children of their own sex, and athletic ability is related to popularity among boys. Emotional adjustment (relative freedom from anxiety), acceptance of others, cooperativeness, and conformity to group standards are also positively correlated with popularity during this period. The expression of inappropriate aggression—aggression that is immature, unprovoked, indirect, and insulting—is negatively correlated with popularity, although according to some studies responding aggressively when provoked is associated with peer acceptance.

In general, popular children are those who are perceived as competent according to the norms of their own group.

> Good adjustment, friendliness, low anxiety, a reasonable level of self-esteem, and some responsiveness and sensitivity to the needs and feelings of other members of the peer group seem to be associated with popularity in most groups. If the group values toughness in males, a boy who is competently aggressive will be popular. If it values athletic prowess or intellectual achievement, competence in those areas will be associated with popularity. In short, the nature of the group and the situation must be considered before any statements can be made about the personality factors in popularity.*

The personality attributes related to popularity vary with sex and age. Thus, among first grade girls popularity is associated with "being quiet and unaggressive," while in the fifth grade the characteristics correlated with girls' popularity are good looks, good sportsmanship, friendliness, and lack of quarrelsomeness. Popular first-grade boys are considered good sports, daring, and good at games; among fifth graders, the most popular boys are good looking, not bashful, and "real boys." Popularity status in childhood is a fairly good predictor of later popularity; those who are popular with their peers during middle childhood are likely to be popular as adolescents.

* E. M. Hetherington and R. D. Parke, *Child Psychology* (New York: McGraw-Hill, 1975), p. 425.

Friendships

In choosing friends, children between the age of 8 and adolescence generally prefer members of their own sex. Between the ages of 6 and 8, sex is ignored in play groupings, but at approximately 8, attitudes seem to change and associations with members of the opposite sex decrease sharply. By the age of 11 or 12, boys and girls in American culture are almost completely segregated from each other in play groups and in social gatherings. "This stage of segregation began with haughty aloofness, became apparent contempt, and active hostility, and then changed to shy withdrawal which seemed to mark the end of this period and the beginning of adolescent heterosexuality after puberty."*

The segregation of the sexes during these years is probably related to sex-typing and to cultural pressures on children to adopt sex-appropriate behavior. As social attitudes and values change, there will undoubtedly be less stress on stereotyped sex roles and patterns of behavior. Among American children in the 1970s there are, however, striking sex differences in play, reading, movie and television preferences, and in vocational choices and aspirations. Boys between the ages of 8 and 11 are principally interested in playing active, vigorous, competitive games involving muscle skills and dexterity, while girls of this age generally engage in quieter, more sedentary activities. Occupational choices also reflect sex-typing, boys choosing such vocations as scientist or pilot and girls aspiring to activities such as teaching, nursing, or social work. Since peers of the same sex are more likely to have the same needs and interests, they are more likely to be satisfying and rewarding friends.

The period of middle childhood is generally marked by more intense friendships rather than by significant increases in numbers of friends. Children's "best friends" are usually from their own neighborhoods or classrooms and possess valued personality characteristics. When asked the reasons for choosing their friends, children in the second grade stress external factors—a nice home, good looks, having money to spend. Sixth-graders, however, emphasize personal characteristics such as friendliness, cheerfulness, and similarity of interests.

Pairs of friends (reciprocated friendships) tend to resemble each other in social maturity, chronological age, height, weight, general intelligence, and educational and occupational goals. Are friends chosen on the basis of *similarity* in personality characteristics, or do opposites attract? There is no clear-cut answer to this question.

* E. H. Campbell, "The Social-Sex Development of Children," *Genetic Psychology Monographs*, 21, no. 4 (1939), 465.

Certainly, capable, friendly, energetic, responsive, outgoing, adventurous children are often attracted to each other, probably because they understand each other better and satisfy each other's needs. Other kinds of children are often attracted to those with these characteristics, but they are usually rejected.

One study yielded some evidence of *complementarity*—opposites attracting—in the reciprocal friendship choices of eighth-grade boys. For example, many attention-seeking boys had friends who were willing to share the limelight and were supportive of them. Among the girls in this same study, there was no evidence of complementarity in friendship choices. Rather, mutual friends were alike on variables such as outgoingness, concern with having a good time, and interest in social activity.

Compared with the friendships of adolescence and adulthood, friendships during middle childhood are more superficial and more unstable; they involve less emotional investment. The foundations are sharing activities, doing things together, doing favors, and getting along easily, rather than more subtle and complex considerations. At this period of development, interests fluctuate rapidly so that "old" friends may no longer provide the kinds of gratifications they provided a short time earlier. Consequently, interests become more crystallized; at the same time, friendships become more emotionally relevant, more stable, and more enduring.

SOCIAL PATTERNS OF ADOLESCENTS

The social relationships of adolescents are more complex and have more ramifications than those of younger children. Adolescents live simultaneously in two worlds, a children's and an adults', in a kind of marginal or overlapping status and not knowing where they belong. All at once they have many new, urgent, and conflicting demands put on them: choosing a vocation, achieving some independence from the family, coping with strong—and often forbidden—sexual impulses. Peers can be of inestimable value in helping the adolescent deal with complex feelings, conflicts, and threatening or suppressed feelings. Intimate adolescent friends feel free to discuss these matters openly and to criticize each other. Consequently, they may learn to modify behavior, tastes, and ideas without painful experiences of disapproval or rejection.

Since adolescents have greater mobility than younger children, their social world broadens and they can maintain friendships over wider geographical areas. Earlier, most of their peers and friends were from their own neighborhood and social-class group, but in high school they are likely to meet boys and girls from other parts of the community and from other ethnic and cultural groups. Furthermore, they are more open to new experiences and new ideas, more flexible in their thinking. Hence, adolescents have many opportunities to acquire new attitudes, customs, and value systems.

Dynamics of Adolescent Groups

A fascinating series of studies conducted by Musafer Sherif and his colleagues is the source of significant insights into group formation, intergroup relations, intergroup tensions, and leadership during adolescence.* The findings of these studies have important implications not just for understanding adolescents but also for understanding group dynamics in general.

A group of middle-class white Protestant boys were taken to a summer camp and divided into two subgroups that were carefully matched in ability and personality characteristics. There was very little contact between the two groups during the five days of the study; they occupied separate cabins and had their own programs of activities with very little adult leadership. Within this short period, clear hierarchical structures emerged in both groups. Leadership and "low man on the totem pole" positions crystallized early. Leaders tended to be highly intelligent, active, sociable, assertive and aggressive boys, although leadership and popularity were only slightly correlated.

Nor did it take long for each group to establish standards and norms. Each group adopted an identifying group nickname, and there was considerable "we-they" discussion. The group members themselves formulated rules, sanctions, and punishments, although these norms were flexible and modifiable as the interests and attitudes of group members changed.

> Emergent hierarchies and shared norms . . . maintain the existence of the group. It does not follow that children have a "natural" propensity for forming structured groups or that they need to share norms with peers in order to survive. Rather, it seems that the incentives and punishments arising from peer interaction itself produce these outcomes; these outcomes, in turn, serve to sustain the group.†

* M. Sherif et al., *Intergroup Conflict and Cooperation: The Robbers Cave Experiment* (Norman: University of Oklahoma Book Exchange, 1961).

† W. W. Hartup, "Peer Interaction and Social Organization," in *Carmichael's Manual of Child Psychology*, 3rd ed., ed. P. H. Mussen (New York: John Wiley & Sons, 1970), p. 371.

Using the same partly naturalistic, partly experimental techniques—that is, dividing a summer camp group into two separate groups—the investigators attempted to make each group a cohesive unit by forcing the members to cooperate in many daily activities, such as securing food and preparing and serving meals. It did not take long for the members of these groups to develop strong feelings of group belonging. Once these feelings had been established, the investigators began to set up competition between the two groups. For example, they arranged competitive games and awarded prizes to the winning team. Under these conditions, tensions between the groups developed rapidly, and the investigators created situations to raise the level of these tensions. They arranged a party and contrived to have one group arrive some time before the other. By the time the second group arrived, the first group had eaten the best refreshments, leaving only the most unappetizing for their rivals. Understandably, hostile feelings increased, the boys called each other names, and they threw food, cups, and other objects at one another.

The investigators then attempted to reduce the intergroup hostilities by eliminating competitive conflict situations and encouraging simple noncompetitive contacts between groups—for example, watching movies together, eating in the same room, and playing in the same area. This attempt backfired, however; putting the groups in close proximity only served to increase their hostilities toward each other.

Only by getting members of the two groups to cooperate did the investigators succeed in reducing these hostilities. They formed an all-star baseball team that included members from both groups and played against a group of boys from a nearby town. The camp truck "unexpectedly" broke down, and all the boys had to cooperate in repairing it so that they could go on a camping trip. After a number of these cooperative ventures, intergroup animosity was considerably reduced and friendships developed between members of the two different groups. In fact, they began to cooperate spontaneously in other situations, and evidences of hostility disappeared.

These investigations give us important information about the function of cooperation and competition in the development of ingroup feelings and intergroup hostility. They also have some practical implications.

> If, for example, the membership of two hostile peer groups can be reshuffled and the newly formed groups induced to function with some common purpose, interpersonal hostility *within* each new group should diminish. Further, if two hostile groups combine to work coop-

eratively toward a superordinate goal, intergroup hostility should be reduced.*

ADOLESCENT CLIQUES AND CROWDS Analyses of peer interactions suggest that there are two basic kinds of groups during adolescence: relatively large crowds and much smaller cliques (generally about one-third the size of the crowd). The crowd is essentially an association of cliques, although an individual may be a clique member but not a crowd member. A clique is generally a small group that includes the individual's best friends and a few other adolescents, usually not more than six or seven. This permits and encourages a higher degree of intimacy and group cohesion, and a great proportion of clique interaction is centered on discussion of basic needs, conflicts, feelings, and ideas. Larger, more organized social activities such as parties are more likely to be crowd functions. With growing maturity during adolescence, the structure of peer groups changes. Dexter Dunphy, a sociologist who has studied adolescent peer groups in depth, notes that structural changes develop in five stages.

> *Stage 1:* Persistence of the preadolescent same-sex cliques into the adolescent period.
> *Stage 2:* Same-sex cliques begin to participate in heterosexual action—often of a superficially antagonistic sort—but these interactions occur only in the security of the group setting where the individual is supported by close friends of his own sex.
> *Stage 3:* High-status members of girl cliques begin to interact on an individual basis with high-status members of boy cliques. This makes the transition to heterosexual cliques while each individual still maintains membership in his same-sex clique.
> *Stage 4:* Reorganization of same-sex cliques and the formation of new heterosexual crowds, made up of heterosexual cliques in close association.
> *Stage 5:* The slow disintegration of the crowd and the formation of cliques consisting of couples who are going steady or engaged.†

Crowd and clique membership in high school is strongly influenced by factors such as social class, educational aspiration (planning to go to college or not), ethnic background, neighborhood, common interests and hobbies, social and personal maturity, and degree of heterosexual interest. Boys' groups are somewhat more democratic and flexible than girls' groups, and athletic skills and overall sociability are more critical considerations.

* Ibid., p. 372.
† D. C. Dunphy, "The Social Structure of Urban Adolescent Peer Groups," *Sociometry*, 26 (1963), 238.

Adolescent Friendships

As we noted earlier, adolescents in our culture often experience doubts, anxieties, and strong resentments. They desperately need friends whom they can trust completely, with whom they can share their complex feelings, conflicts, and secrets without fear of misunderstanding or rejection. For these reasons, adolescent friendships are typically more intimate, more honest and open, and involve more intense feelings than those of earlier periods. Consequently, they contribute more to the individual's development and, more specifically, may play a critical role in helping adolescents to define their capabilities.

> The particular advantage of the adolescent friendship is that it offers a climate for growth and self-knowledge that the family is not equipped to offer, and that very few persons can provide for themselves. Friendship engages, discharges, cultivates, and transforms the most acute passions of the adolescent, and so allows the youngster to confront and master them. Because it carries so much of the burden of adolescent growth, friendship acquires at this time a pertinence and intensity it has never had before nor (in many cases) will ever have again.*

Friends "examine themselves, placing in common their experiences, their plans, their ambitions, and their most intimate secrets. In the true sense, they explain themselves to each other, and in so doing, each explains himself to himself."†

The nature of friendship relationships changes during the period of adolescence. Early adolescent friendships are not much different from those of middle childhood; they are relatively superficial, involving doing favors for each other, sharing activities, and simply getting along well. By midadolescence, relationships are "mutual, interactive, emotionally interdependent; the personality of the other and the other's response to the self become the central themes of friendship."‡ During this period, adolescents reveal a distinctive talent for friendship. More than at earlier or later ages, the individual is flexible and ready to change—and is convinced that by conscious, deliberate effort he or she *can* change.

Understandably then, the major criteria adolescents use in se

* E. Douvan and J. Adelson, *The Adolescent Experience* (New York: John Wiley & Sons, 1966), p. 174.

† P. A. Osterrieth, "Adolescence: Some Psychological Aspects," in *Adolescence: Psychological Perspectives*, ed. G. Caplan and S. Lebovici (New York: Basic Books, 1969), p. 19.

‡ Douvan and Adelson, *The Adolescent Experience*, p. 188.

lecting friends are loyalty, understanding, trustworthiness, respect for confidences, and supportiveness in emotional crises. Mutual friends are likely to resemble each other in such personality and social characteristics as age, intelligence, socioeconomic status, shared interests, and career goals. While friendships may sometimes involve complementarity—an extroverted adolescent girl may have a shy, inhibited friend—similarities are generally more prominent than differences. Because friendships at this age are very intense, they may be fragile and more easily endangered than those of most adults, who make more modest demands on their friends.

In later adolescence, as heterosexual relationships develop, there is less exclusive reliance on friends of the same sex. Sharing confidences with someone is still important, but there is a less passionate quality to friendship relations; there is a greater, more objective emphasis on the personality and talents of friends and on how interesting and stimulating they are. More mature friendship relationships involve a great degree of tolerance for individual differences; as the adolescent begins to develop a firm sense of ego identity, he or she becomes less intensely dependent on identification with close friends.

There are notable sex differences in adolescent friendship patterns. Girls' friendships are generally deeper and more interdependent and involve more frequent contacts; their relationships reveal their greater nurturance needs and ability to maintain intimate relationships. In contrast, boys place relatively more stress on the results of friendships, such as having a congenial companion, someone with whom to share common interests.

Heterosexual Relations during Adolescence

During the junior high school years, boys and girls are at distinctly different levels of biological and social maturity. Some girls are interested in boys, but their male contemporaries do not generally reciprocate their interest. At this age, girls are much more concerned with social life and heterosexual behavior than boys are.

All this changes by about the sophomore year of high school, when boys begin to catch up with girls in maturity and in interest in the opposite sex. Boys' and girls' interests now begin to complement each other, and they pay more attention to one another. During the period of initial heterosexual relationships, adolescents are still pretty much involved in finding themselves, in achieving ego identity. They are still preoccupied with themselves and their own problems and are unlikely to become emotionally involved with members of the opposite sex. Consequently, there is frequently a superficial or gamelike quality to heterosexual interactions. Heterosexual group activities at this stage provide opportunities to learn ways of relating to opposite sex peers gradually, in settings that have the security provided by the presence of familiar same-sex peers.

Gradually, with greater experience with heterosexual cliques, increased personal maturity, and greater self-confidence, heterosexual relations become more mature. When the adolescent has achieved a clearer sense of identity, generally in late adolescence, he or she can form genuine relationships with others. These are based not only on sexual attraction but also on shared trust and confidence together with concern about the interests and well-being of the other person.

Compared with other cultures, American culture has traditionally been rather restrictive about sexual expression among children and adolescents. Standards of sexual morality and sexual behavior appear to be changing rapidly, however. Today's adolescents believe that new sexual standards have been set, but they do not view the change as a lowering of morals. Rather, they see their attitudes and approaches as more honest and open than those of earlier generations.

Most older adolescents and young people consider premarital intercourse acceptable when the couple is engaged, is going steady, or has an understanding about getting married. In the United States, 80 percent of adolescent boys and 72 percent of adolescent girls agree that "its all right for young people to have sex before getting married if they are in love with each other." Promiscuity is not generally sanctioned; in fact, the vast majority of adolescents disapprove of premarital sexual relationships between people who are merely "casually attracted" or "good friends." Among adolescent girls, 75 percent maintain that "I wouldn't want to have sex with a boy unless I loved him." Compared with older adolescents, younger ones are more conservative and hold less permissive attitudes toward premarital sexual relationships.

Although today's adolescents talk more openly and freely about sex than adolescents of a generation ago,

> there is little evidence of an increased preoccupation with sex, as many parents and other adults seem to think. Indeed, it may well be that the average adolescent of today is less preoccupied and concerned with sex than prior generations of young people, including his or her parents when they were the same age. Greater acceptance of sex as a natural part of life may well lead to less preoccupation than did anxious concern in an atmosphere of secrecy and suppression. Most

contemporary adolescents (87 percent) agree that "all in all, I think my head is pretty well together as far as sex is concerned."*

Changes in adolescents' attitudes toward sex have been accompanied by radical changes in their sexual behavior. Although the incidence of masturbation has not changed appreciably in the last few decades, there is greater objectivity and less anxiety and guilt about the practice. The percentage of adolescents who engage in premarital sexual intercourse has increased significantly over this same period. A survey of a representative sample of adolescents between 13 and 19 years of age, published in 1973, documented the fact that 44 percent of boys and 30 percent of girls have sexual intercourse before they are sixteen; by age 19, the figures have increased to 72 percent (boys) and 57 percent (girls). Among college students, 82 percent of the men and 56 percent of the women have had sexual intercourse. In their parents' generation, only 3 percent of females and 39 percent of males had intercourse before the age of 16; less than 20 percent of females and 72 percent of males had premarital intercourse by age 19. Of course, these are overall statistics, and there are wide differences among groups within the population. For example, the incidence of sexual intercourse among college students is highest in eastern and West Coast colleges and among those attending "elite" private colleges and universities; it is lowest among those attending midwestern and church-related institutions. Politically liberal students tend to be more permissive with respect to sexual behavior, while those who are more conservative politically are also more conservative in their sexual attitudes and behavior.

Adolescent Values and Beliefs

We hear a great deal nowadays about adolescents and youth being "in revolt" and creating "a counterculture." To a great extent, this view is a carryover from the turbulent 1960s when

significant minorities of young people became increasingly disillusioned by a society they viewed as unjust, cruel, violent, hypocritical, superficial, impersonal, overly competitive, or, in the broadest sense of the term, immoral. They reacted to this state of affairs in a variety of ways. Some became social dropouts; others began vigorous efforts to institute social change—efforts that ran the gamut from conventional political activity within the system to extreme revolutionary tactics.†

* J. J. Conger, *Adolescence and Youth* (New York: Harper & Row, Publishers, 1977) p. 283.
† Ibid., p. 538.

Average adolescents in the 1970s are much less involved in political and social movements and hold more traditional values than their counterparts in the 1960s. In recent surveys, very few students classify themselves as "far left" or "far right," and a majority label themselves "middle of the road." Campus demonstrations have practically disappeared, and the influence of militant radicals is much less apparent. This does not mean that today's college students are satisfied with the political system of the United States. Most of them believe that as nation we need some fundamental reforms of social institutions, political parties, and the political system, but they do not advocate radical actions to bring about change.

Many of the new values that became prominent in youth culture in the 1960s—for example, the liberalized attitudes toward sex, the so-called new morality—are being maintained and, in fact, are accepted by greater numbers of young people. In 1969, 43 percent of college students stated that they would "welcome more acceptance of sexual freedom"; this increased to 56 percent in 1971 and 61 percent in 1973. The 1960s trend toward considering sexual behavior a matter of personal decision, rather than a subject for laws or socially imposed moral codes, has also gained momentum. Since 1969 there has been a marked increase in the percentage of students who do not regard abortion, relations between consenting homosexuals, or having children outside of marriage as morally wrong. Having children is increasingly seen as a matter of individual choice rather than a duty to society or an indispensible personal value.

Among the adolescents of the 1960s, the values ranked as having the greatest importance were love and kindness, friendship, individual freedom, opportunities for self-expression and self-fulfillment, and treating people as individuals (rather than as blacks or whites, men or women, lower or upper class, heterosexuals or homosexuals, Americans or foreigners). These values have been retained by the adolescents of the 1970s, and in many cases their importance has been augmented.

Most youth appear to have greater concern than their parents do (or than their parents did as adolescents) with racial and socioeconomic discrimination, preservation of the environment, and the need for improved education. Compared with their parents, adolescents are much more likely to perceive discrimination against minorities and to favor increased school integration and having minority-group members as neighbors. "In their attitudes, most adolescents seem to be reflecting flexibility, tolerance, and lack of prejudice as much as, or more than, crusading zeal."*

---

* Ibid.

What is perhaps most impressive is youths' widespread concern with humanitarian values and their pervasive desire to help create a world in which there is more true friendship, love, and kindness, greater individual freedom, and equality of opportunity for everyone.

> In brief, the average contemporary adolescent appears to be relatively more ready than his more self-conscious predecessors of earlier generations to put into practice a philosophy of "live and let live" and a pragmatic idealism. More than earlier generations, he appears to be a sophisticated and critical exponent of the art of the possible—not illusioned, but not disillusioned either.*

DEVELOPMENTAL PSYCHOLOGY AND HUMAN WELFARE

Most psychologists share youth's concern with the human condition and with the improvement of society; they would like to contribute to the task of making this a better world to live in. Developmental psychology should play a significant role in achieving this goal. Many of society's problems have their roots in *individuals'* psychological development and early socialization. Investigations of the psychological antecedents of social problems yield information that has implications for eliminating or alleviating these problems. For example, as we learned earlier, developmental psychologists have discovered that children's cognitive deficiencies are in large part the products of extremely unstimulating environmental experiences in infancy and early childhood (see chapter 3). These findings are very useful in formulating programs of positive social actions—specifically, intensive programs to stimulate early cognitive development among disadvantaged children. Some of these programs have proven to be very effective (see chapter 3).

As another example, consider again the social problems, such as juvenile delinquency, we discussed briefly in chapter 5. Well-designed studies of delinquents and matched controls demonstrate that poor parent-child relationships and parental rejection, physical punishment, and erratic discipline are major antecedent factors in juvenile delinquency. Most delinquents feel rejected by their parents, deprived, insecure, jealous of their siblings, uncomfortable about family tensions and parental misconduct, and thwarted in their needs for independence and self-expression. Delinquents do not readily identify with their parents, and partly for this reason they

* Ibid.

may fail to acquire acceptable patterns of social behavior. In brief, their delinquency may be viewed as the result of certain kinds of social learning and socialization experiences that lead them to behave in ways detrimental to their own and others' welfare and happiness.

Again, however, research findings allow us to sound an optimistic note. Delinquent behavior, like other maladaptive behavior, does not develop inevitably, and if it does develop it is not necessarily fixed and immutable. Like most other forms of maladjustment, delinquency consists of acquired—not biologically determined—patterns of responses, and these are modifiable. The findings about the childhood antecedents of delinquency may be useful in developing psychological, social welfare, and educational programs to aid parents in establishing better relationships with their children. At the same time, delinquents (and potential delinquents) must be helped to learn more appropriate and effective ways of handling their personal problems.

In similar ways, investigations of the development and modification of highly aggressive behavior have great practical social utility, providing convincing evidence that, with relatively little training, parents can change their child-rearing practices so that their children's aggressive outbursts diminish. Research on group formation among adolescents demonstrated that hostility and competition between groups can be relieved by getting members of competing groups to cooperate in achieving a common goal. Applying these findings, Elliot Aronson created a situation in which children came to like each other better and became less prejudiced against peers of different ethnic and racial backgrounds. He divided several fifth-grade classrooms into six-person cooperative groups and gave each group an assignment. Each of the six children in the group received a small part of this assignment; in order to complete the entire assignment they had to cooperate with each other, to teach and to learn from each other. One lesson involved the life of the famous publisher Joseph Pulitzer. The group was presented with a six-paragraph biography, each paragraph covering a major aspect of Pulitzer's life (his immigration to the United States, his childhood, his later success). Each child in the group learned one paragraph and taught the contents to the others in the group. The results of these experiments were striking. The children who worked together came to like each other better, their mutual affections cutting across ethnic and racial lines. In addition, they reported liking school better and learned the material better than children in traditional classrooms where children compete with each other for grades and teacher approval.

The Investigation of Prosocial Behavior

For the past decade, the author focused his research attention on the development of prosocial behavior, actions intended to aid or benefit another person or a group of people without the actor's anticipation of external rewards. Data on child-rearing practices that foster generosity, altruism, sympathy, and consideration of others, (reviewed in chapter 5) demonstrate that modeling and identification are critical processes underlying the development of these prosocial behaviors. The parents of altruistic, generous, and highly considerate children are warm and nurturant and, at the same time, good models of prosocial behavior. They use reasoning in their discipline and maintain high standards for their children. Long-term positive relationships with altruistic models is conducive to the development of altruistic behavior. Such findings are potentially applicable by many different agents of socialization: parents, educators, clergy, media people. For example, parents who want to raise prosocial children or increase the frequency of prosocial activities among their children may be advised to employ time-honored practices, including modeling the helping and sharing behaviors clearly and frequently; reasoning with their children in disciplining them; encouraging the children to reflect on their own and others' feelings, emotions, and expectations; maintaining high standards for the child and being explicit about these; and assigning responsibility for others early.

Modeling of prosocial acts by television characters has also proven effective in raising the level of children's socially positive behavior. Children readily copy cooperative, sympathetic, sharing, and understanding actions after they see these portrayed in television programs. It may be concluded that conscientious, socially responsible television programming can help increase the incidence of helping and sharing among child viewers by presenting more examples of heroes behaving prosocially and, at the same time, by decreasing portrayals of violence and aggression.

These findings on prosocial behavior are important in themselves, but even more significantly, the studies are models of the kind of research that is urgently needed to understand the determinants of positive, socially desirable behavior. Without such understanding, it is not possible to devise methods of facilitating the acquisition and augmentation of such behavior.

The great promise of developmental psychology is its potential contributions to the improvement of the human condition and human relationships. To fulfill this promise, developmental psychologists must continue to investigate ways of reducing maladjustment and socially undesirable behaviors, such as aggression, delinquency, and prejudice. In addition, however, we must intensify and improve research on how constructive social actions can be fostered. Fortunately, the movement toward more research on prosocial behavior is gaining considerable momentum; in the near future, our knowledge in this area will undoubtedly be greatly expanded.

Index

Adolescents and adolescence
  cliques, 112
  cross-cultural study of, 11, 63–65
  and formal operations stage,
    40–41
  peer-group influence during,
    89–91
  physiological determinants of, 3
  popularity in, 107
  social patterns of, 109–18
    dynamics, 110–12
    friendship, 113–14
    heterosexual behavior, 114–16
    values and beliefs, 116–18
Age changes, 3–4
Aggression, 4, 5, 6
  determinants of, 57
  as effect of television, 96–97
  family interaction and, 79–80
  modification of, 100–101, 118–19
  negative correlation of popularity
    with, 105
  peer influences on, 87–88
Ainsworth, Mary, 70
Anxiety, 4
Arapesh people, sex typing among,
  63
Aronson, Elliot, 119

Attachment, in mother-child rela-
    tionship, 68–73
  and cognitive/emotional char-
    acteristics, 70–71
  and sense of trust, 71–72
Authoritarian parents, 77, 78
Authoritative parents, 77, 78–79
Autistic children, 56

Baumrind, Diana, 77
Bayley Scales of Infant Develop-
    ment, 42, 43
Behavior. See also Social behavior,
    development of
  modification of, 98–101, 118–20
  prosocial, 120–21
  situational determinants of, 93–94
Biological determinants of person-
    ality, 53, 54–57
  genetic influences, 54–56
  maturation rate, 58–59
  testosterone secretions, 57
  thyroid effect, 57
Bronfenbrenner, Urie, 89
Bruner, Jerome, 24–25

Center for Cognitive Studies (Har-
    vard), 24–25

Child-rearing techniques
  effect of different types of home
    atmosphere, 76–79
  long-term effects of early mater-
    nal treatment, 74–75
  mother-child attachment, 68–73
  in second year, 75–76
China, family orientation in, 89
Class inclusion, 36
Cliques, 112
Cognitive development, 5, 16
  Piaget's stages of, 4, 27–28, 35–41
Compensatory education, 49–52
Competition, study of, 4
  among adolescents, 111–12
  socialization of, 62
Conditioning, 17–18
  of infants, 25–26
Conscience, 84–86
Cooperation, study of, 4
  among adolescents, 111–12
Crime, 5
Cultural-group membership, as
    determinant of personality,
    53

Delinquency, juvenile, 5, 86, 118–19
  modification of, 119–20
Dependency, study of, 4
  during preschool years, 106
  situational determinants of, 97–98
Deprivation, social, 97–98
Depth, perception of, 23
Dunphy, Dexter, 112

Economic deprivation, IQ and,
    48–52
Ego identity, 82–83
Environment
  as determinant of behavior, 93–94
  as determinant of dependency,
    97–98
  as determinant of intelligence,
    47–48
  personality development and,
    13–15, 55–56, 59–67
  adolescence, 63–65
  effect of different types of
    home atmosphere, 76–79
  and modification of parent-
    child relationship, 99
  reduction of cognitive defi-
    ciency of economically

disadvantaged children,
    48–52
  sex typing, 63
  sexuality, 65
  social-class differences, 65–67
Erikson, Erik, 19, 72, 82
Experimental techniques, 7–8,
    102–3

Family, personality development
    and, 53–54, 86
  child-rearing techniques during
    second year, 75–76
  conscience development, 84–86
  effects of different types of home
    atmosphere, 76–79
  family interactions and aggressive
    behavior, 79–80
  identification, 80–84
  long-term effects of early mater-
    nal treatment, 74–75
  mother-child relationship, 68–73
Fels longitudinal study, 92
Films, and behavioral modification,
    101
Flavell, John, 30
Formal operations stage of cogni-
    tive development, 40–41
Freud, Sigmund, 82
Friendship
  adolescent, 113–14
  in middle childhood, 108–9
  during preschool years, 104–5
Frustration, 94–97

Genetics
  as determinant of intelligence, 45,
    46–47
  as determinant of personality,
    54–56, 57–58
  and development, 13–15
Ghetto children, cognitive ca-
    pabilities of, 5
Grammar, 32–34
Growth rate of infants, 1–2

Harlow, Harry, 74
Heber, Rick, 49
Heredity
  as determinant of intelligence, 3,
    45, 46–47
  and development, 13–15

Hopi Indians
  identification among, 81
  socialization among, 62

Identification, 80–84
  research on, 83–84
  sex-role preferences, 84
  sex typing, 81–82
Identity crisis, 82
Infants, study of, 19–20. *See also*
    Neonates
  development of, 12–13
  growth rate, 1–2
  intelligence tests for, 42–44
  language acquisition and cogni-
    tive skills, 16
  mother-child relationship, 68–73
  posture and locomotive develop-
    ment, 16 illus.
Inhelder, Barbel, 40–41
Institute of Human Development
    (Berkeley), 77
Intelligence, development of, 41–52
Intelligence tests, 41–45
  Bayley Scales of Infant Develop-
    ment, 42, 43
  and economically disadvantaged
    children, 48–52
  factors relating to performance,
    45–52
    environmental factors, 45,
      47–48
    hereditary factors, 45, 46–67
  for infants, 42–44
  IQ stability and change, 44–45
  nature of, 42–45
  predictive value of, 42, 45
  Stanford-Binet intelligence test,
    43–44, 47, 51
  Wechsler intelligence test, 44, 51
IQ. *See* Intelligence tests
Iran, mother-child attachment in, 73
Israel, personality development in
    kibbutzim, 10, 62, 64, 89

Japan
  identification in, 81
  socialization in, 61–62
Juvenile delinquency. *See* Delin-
    quency, juvenile

Language development, 16, 29–35
  grammar, 32–34

innate capability for, 32–34
  phonemes, 31–32
  psycholinguistics, 31, 34
Learning, 17–19
  classical conditioning, 17–18
  language as base of, 29
  in neonates and infants, 23–26
  observational learning, 18
  operant conditioning, 18

Maturation, 3–4, 15
  as determinant of personality,
    58–59
Mead, Margaret, 63, 64
Memory, development of, 39–40
  in neonates and infants, 23–26
Mitosis, 12
Moods, behavior and, 98
Moral development, 85–86
Mother-child relationship, person-
    ality development and, 68–75
Mundugamor tribe
  sex typing among, 63
  identification and, 81

Neonates, characteristics of, 20–28.
    See also Infants, study of
  changes in form and proportion
    of body, 21 illus.
  learning and memory in, 23–26
  neonatal needs, 20–21
  physical growth, 20
  Piaget on infancy, 26–28
  sensory and perceptual abilities,
    21–23
Nutrition, intelligence and, 48

Observation technique, 6–7, 8–9,
    102
Operant conditioning, 18
Operational stage of cognitive de-
    velopment, 16
Ordering (seriating), 36–37

Palmer, Francis, 51–52
Papousek, Hanus, 25–26
Parent-child relationship, 8–9. *See
    also* Mother-child relation-
    ship
  in adolescence, 90–91
  child-rearing techniques during
    second year, 75–76

Parent-child relationship (*cont.*)
  and conscience development,
    84–86
  effect of home environment on,
    76–79
  environmental modification, 99
  and identification, 81–82
  and juvenile delinquency, 118–19
  and positive modification of be-
    havior, 100–101
  styles of, 77–79
Patterson, Gerald, 79, 100–101
Pavlov, Ivan, 17–18
Peers
  as agents of personality and be-
    havior modification, 99, 101
  social interaction with, 103–6
  socialization through, 86–91
    aggressiveness, 87–88
    cross-cultural comparison, 89
    peer-group influence during ad-
      olescence, 89–91
    peers as models, 88–89
    sex typing, 87
Perception, children's, 4, 21–23
Permissive parents, personality de-
    velopment and, 77, 78
Personality development, 17, 53–67
  biological determinants, 53,
    54–59
  cultural determinants, 53, 59–67
  familial influence, 68–86
  modification of personality,
    98–101
  personality, defined, 53
  situational determinants, 54
  socialization determinants, 53–54,
    59, 60–62
  stability of personality char-
    acteristics, 91–98
    frustration and aggression,
      94–97
    situational determinants of be-
      havior, 93–94
    situational determinants of de-
      pendency, 97–98
Physical growth, 1–2, 4, 20
Piaget, Jean
  analysis of intelligence as adapt-
    ive behavior, 42
  on infancy, 26–28
  on language and early develop-
    ment, 30
  on observational learning, 24

  and stages of cognitive develop-
    ment, 4, 16, 29, 30, 35–37,
    40–41
Popularity
  in childhood and adolescence,
    107
  during middle childhood, 107
  during preschool years, 105–6
Prenatal development, 12, 13, 15, 21
    illus.
Preschool years, social behavior
    during, 103–6
Prosocial behavior, 85–86
Psycholinguistics, 31, 34

Race, IQ differentials and, 47–48
Research methods in child psychol-
    ogy, 6–11
  cross-cultural approach, 10–11
  cross-sectional approach, 10
  experimentation, 7–8, 102–3
  longitudinal approach, 9–10
  objective measurement, 6
  observation, 6–7, 8–9, 102
  and parent-child relations, 8–9
  for study of social behavior,
    102–3
Reversibility, concept of, 38

Samoa, adolescence in, 10, 64
Schizophrenia, determinants of, 56
Sensorimotor phase of cognitive de-
    velopment, 27–30
Sensory abilities in neonates, 21–23
Sex differences, social conflicts and,
    106
Sex grouping, friendships and,
    108–9
Sex typing, 63, 81–82, 87
Sexuality, adolescence and, 111–16,
    117
Sherif, Musafer, 110
Slobin, D. I., 33–34
Social behavior, development of,
    102–21
  of adolescents, 109–18
    adolescence and friendships,
      113–14
    dynamics of adolescents, 110–12
    and heterosexual behavior,
      114–16
    values and beliefs, 116–18
  in middle childhood, 106–9

in preschool years, 103–6
study of, 102–3
Social-class differences, personality
determinants and, 65–67
Socialization
as determinant of personality,
53–54, 59, 60–62
peers as agents of, 86–91
Solidity, perception of, 22–23
Soviet Union, peer orientation in,
89
Stanford-Binet intelligence test,
43–44, 47, 51
Superego, 82, 84–86

Tchambuli tribe, sex typing among,
63
Television, effect of, on aggression,
96–97
Temperament, genetic influence on,
15
Testosterone, aggressiveness and, 57
Thought, development of, 35–41
concrete operations phase, 38–39
formal operations phase, 40–41

memory, 39–40
preoperational thought, 35–37
Thyroid activity, personality and,
57
Trust
critical period for formation of,
19
and mother-child attachment,
71–72
Twin studies
of intelligence determinants,
46–47
of personality development,
55–56

Values, adolescent, 116–18
Verbal mediation, 30
Violence, 5
televised, and aggression, 96–97
Vygotsky, 30

Wechsler intelligence test, 44, 51
Welfare, developmental psychology
and, 118–21

DATE DUE